The Spokesman
Revolutions
Edited by Ken Coates
Published by Spokesman for the Bertrand Russell Peace Foundation

Spokesman 104 2009

CONTENTS

Editorial
1 Drone Wars in Pakistan 3 *Paul Rogers*
2 Blowback or Frame-up in Lancashire? 5 *Ken Coates*

Two, Three, Many Revolutions … 9 *Peter Linebaugh*

Keynes and the G20 – Altering the World Money

1 On Redistribution of Income 18 *Michael Barratt Brown*
2 On Bretton Woods 25 *Stuart Holland*
3 Unfinished Business 31 *Ken Coates*
4 How to Do It 33 *Zhou Xiaochuan*

Apartheid in Palestine 38 *John Dugard*

The Russell Tribunal on Palestine

1 Until When? 44 *Nurit Peled*
2 Russell Tribunals 47 *Ken Coates*
3 The Situation in Palestine 50 *Richard Falk*

Viva Palestina 70 *George Galloway MP*
Licence to Torture 75 *Tony Simpson*
I Disown this Government 81 *Bryan Gould*
Reviews 85 *Michael Barratt Brown, Peter Jackson, Richard Minns, Christopher Gifford, Henry McCubbin, Abi Rhodes, Joyce Chumbley*

Dossier 101

Cover: The Lewes Pound is a complementary currency redeemable by participating traders. It's obtainable from www.thelewespound.org.

ISSN 1367 7748   Printed by the Russell Press Ltd., Nottingham   ISBN 978 0 85124 768 7

Subscriptions
Institutions £35.00
Individuals £20.00 (UK)
£25.00 (ex UK)

Back issues available on request

A CIP catalogue record for this book is available from the British Library

Published by the
Bertrand Russell Peace Foundation Ltd.,
Russell House
Bulwell Lane
Nottingham NG6 0BT
England
Tel. 0115 9784504
email:
elfeuro@compuserve.com
www.spokesmanbooks.com
www.russfound.org

Editorial Board:
Michael Barratt Brown
Ken Coates
John Daniels
Ken Fleet
Stuart Holland
Tony Simpson

Bertrand Russell at Routledge

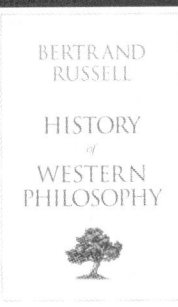

History of Western Philosophy
Illustrated Gift Edition

Sixty years after its first publication, Bertrand Russell's monumental *History of Western Philosophy* is one of the best-selling philosophy books of all time.

Now in a special gift edition, and featuring an exquisite colour plates section and a brand new foreword by Anthony Gottlieb, this is a dazzlingly unique exploration of the works of significant philosophers throughout the ages and a definitive must-have title that deserves a revered place on every bookshelf.

'**Beautiful and luminous prose, not merely classically clear but scrupulously honest.**' – *Isaiah Berlin*

'A great philosopher's lucid and magisterial look at the history of his own subject, wonderfully readable and enlightening.' – *The Observer*

March 2009: 234x156: 560pp • Hb: 978-0-415-47881-6: **£30.00**

The home of more of Bertrand Russell's works than any other English language publisher, in 2009 Routledge will be making its complete Bertrand Russell backlist available in the Routledge Classics series.

New to Routledge Classics in March 2009:

ABC of Relativity • *An Outline of Philosophy* • *The Basic Writings of Bertrand Russell*
Bertrand Russell's Best • *Human Knowledge: Its Scope and Limits*
Marriage and Morals • *Mortals and Others* • *Our Knowledge of the External World*
Philosophical Essays • *The Scientific Outlook* • *Unpopular Essays*

Routledge Classics: Get Inside a Great Mind

For more information, a full catalogue or to order titles online visit
www.routledge.com/classics/new.asp or email us at
classics@routledge.com Also available at all good bookshops.

Editorial
1. Drone Wars in Pakistan

The phrase 'war on terror' might have been quietly dropped from the United States' military lexicon – to be replaced (according to a memo to Pentagon staff) by 'overseas contingency operation'. But it is clear that to some degree there is continuity in practice in the tactics being pursued by the coalition in Afghanistan and Pakistan. An example is the relatively little reported campaign in western Pakistan characterised by what (in another euphemism) are commonly termed 'drone incidents', but which would be better called air-raids.

The term 'drone' has a serviceable analytical use, but the suggestion it conveys – of a very small pilot-less aircraft that is more of a scaled-up version of a model aircraft – is misleading as a description of what is happening in parts of Pakistan. For the technology of the 'drone', which is developing at an extraordinary rate, is as sophisticated as its effects are becoming more intensive and destructive.

The present reality of these 'drone' deployments is that United States forces are flying large and heavily armed aircraft over Pakistan for virtually every hour of every day, frequently accompanied by actual attacks. These air-raids have killed hundreds of people, many of them civilians, and including scores of women and children.

Three aspects of this major development in the war are worthy of note: the size and power of the weapons being used, the rapid increase in their use, and the impact in terms of civilian casualties ...

The weapon of choice for United States forces was until recently the Predator, manufactured by General Atomics. The much larger and more powerful MQ-9 Reaper is now becoming their favourite. The Reaper's turboprop engine is nearly eight times as powerful as the Predator; it carries fifteen times the weapons load and yet travels three times more quickly.

Because these planes have no pilots and are operated remotely, often by technicians at bases in the United States, there is a huge 'weight gain'. This, combined with the sheer size of the Reapers, means that they can easily carry a range of weapons on a par with a conventional strike aircraft.

A recent version of the Reaper has a wingspan of over twenty-five metres (about the same as a Boeing 737 passenger-jet), and can carry sufficient fuel to stay airborne for thirty-four hours. If fitted with two drop-tanks and 300 kilograms of weapons, it can fly a forty-two-hour sortie; as pilot fatigue is not an issue, shifts of operators can be used to sustain this length of time in the air.

In practice, however, bombing attacks are more likely to be undertaken by Reapers with a much shorter range, and carrying more weapons. These can include Hellfire air-to-ground missiles, Paveway laser-guided bombs, or GBU-38 Joint Direct Attack Munitions (JDAMs).

The Reaper is a bomber in all but name. A comment in September 2006 on the designation of this 'unmanned aerial vehicle' (UAV) from the then chief-of-staff of the United States Air Force (USAF), General T Michael Moseley, is indicative of official attitudes: 'We've moved from using UAVs primarily in intelligence, surveillance and reconnaissance roles before Operation Iraqi Freedom, to a true hunter role with the Reaper'. An even better indication of its growing role is that, in 2008, the New York Air National Guard 174th fighter wing began to make the change from flying F-16 strike aircraft to 'flying' Reapers.

A recent customer for the Reaper is Britain's Royal Air Force, which has deployed the aircraft in Afghanistan since autumn 2007. Its initial deployment was as an unarmed reconnaissance vehicle, but the armed variant is now in use. The Ministry of Defence (MoD) acknowledges the MQ-9's '[complementary] mission' to be 'a persistent hunter-killer against emerging targets to achieve joint force commander objectives'. The MoD has, however, been notably reticent about publicising actual cases where the Predator has engaged in combat, or about any casualties resulting from this.

These military and technical advances, in the context of the difficulties experienced by western coalition forces in Afghanistan in the war against the Taliban, help explain why the escalation in the number of air-strikes in Pakistan (regarded as the source of much Taliban activity and weaponry) has been rapid.

US forces struck just twice in 2006, three times in 2007 and seven times in the first eight months of 2008. A surge in the last four months of 2008 saw twenty-nine air-raids, and there were fourteen between January and 8 April 2009. Pakistani sources assess the number killed over this near forty-months period at 701, including 14 al Qaeda leaders; 152 of these have lost their lives this year. These sources also claim that the great majority of people killed are civilian, though US military sources often dispute this.

The pattern here is that the Pentagon or US spokespersons closer to the action tend to discount claims of civilian casualties immediately after a raid, only for independent evidence later to appear that confirms the initial local reports. It is therefore plausible in many cases to be sceptical of the denials …

It is also relevant that the air war in Pakistan has accelerated in a manner largely unrecognised in the western media, though this is widely covered in the Middle East and South-West Asia. This goes a long way to explain the anti-western mood in Pakistan, and the difficulty that the current government in Islamabad has in supporting US actions …

Paul Rogers

Paul Rogers is Professor of Peace Studies at Bradford University. His full text is available online (opendemocracy.net). This shortened version is reprinted with grateful acknowledgements.

* * *

2. Blowback or Frame-up in Lancashire?

British police raided a string of addresses on April 8th and 9th in Liverpool, Manchester and Clitheroe (Lancashire) alleging widespread faults in the system of visa allocations for Pakistani students, and claiming that a number of arrests had become necessary in order to uproot a potential terrorist cell. In fact, twelve arrests were made. Eleven involved Pakistani citizens. Bob Quick, the head of Specialist Operations at the Metropolitan Police, became the object of ferocious criticism in the press, because he had carried a top-secret folder under his arm when entering Downing Street. This enabled enthusiastic reporters to take photographs of the summary of the police game-plan, which, it was said, risked compromising the projected operation for the suppression of terrorism. This, therefore, had to be brought slightly forward, apparently to its detriment. The Prime Minister claimed that the police were foiling 'a very big terrorist plot'.

We have seen some of these very big plots before, and they have done something to encourage very big agnosticism about various elements of the war on terror. We shall see how long it takes to charge any of the arrested men, or to release them with or without fulsome apologies, or even compensation for wrongful arrest.

The newspapers cannot be blamed for not knowing how seriously to take police allegations at this stage of their enquiries. It is perfectly possible that all of those detained are wholly or partly guilty, or even completely innocent. But then again, this may not be the reason for the arrests, which certainly revive the jitters among those of a nervous disposition.

We had occasion to warn in *Spokesman No. 99*, before the remarkable victory of Barack Obama in the American Presidential elections, that the

Obama team might, given the chance, authorise an ugly extension of the Afghan war into Pakistan. This was already beginning as a series of illicit raids. We were concerned about the effects of the incursion of Drones into Pakistani airspace, and the increasingly frequent strikes on alleged Pakistani terrorists. Once again, the facts of these cases are veiled in a persistent fog, which includes no small amount of misinformation.

We do not even know whether Osama bin Laden is in fact alive. It would hardly be surprising if all those bombs in all those caves had succeeded in translating him to a different plane of existence. We do know that there are large numbers of Afghans and Pakistanis with substantial grievances against the American and Allied incursions, first in Afghanistan, and now, increasingly, in Pakistan. As we said last year, this is a sinister dimension of the new situation, especially for Gordon Brown. 'For him, Pakistan is not simply a distant country with exotic customs. He has got Pakistan at home as well.' Were the arrests in Lancashire a preliminary recognition of this fact? Or were they a repetition of the dreary recital of scaremongering, false alarms to which we have become increasingly accustomed?

We have already published the most revealing statement by Barack Obama from the Woodrow Wilson Centre, on the 1st August 2007. He promised to 'turn the page'. The first of five elements he promised to confront involved 'getting out of Iraq and on to the right battlefield in Afghanistan and Pakistan'. For emphasis, he promised to take the fight to the terrorists in Afghanistan and Pakistan. Is it now to be claimed that the fight will also be taken, beyond Pakistan, to Manchester, Liverpool and Clitheroe?

There are very large numbers of armed men who have been indoctrinated in the arts of 'taking the fight' here, there and everywhere. Where will they be going next? Which other British communities will fall into their remit? How well justified will be their efforts to suppress terrorism, and how many mistakes will be made in the process? These are very worrying questions. If the war is going to Pakistan, there are bound to be citizens in Britain with Pakistani antecedents, who are likely to regard this as a matter of profound concern.

Before the police squads drill, and the intelligence communities marshal their theories, is it not sensible to ask the question, do we really want to conduct a war in Afghanistan or Pakistan? Is it really wise to alienate a substantial part of our population? Prominent Government Ministers sing from a dreary hymn sheet about the need to root out extremists among the immigrant population. Why don't they address the question of what is seeding extremism, and what actions might foster moderation among the unfortunate people who suffer from all these wars and punitive expeditions?

Might not the cessation of terrorist bombing raids on weddings and other civil reunions be a help?

Ken Coates

Postscript: On 21 April, after this editorial was written, nine more of the 12 men arrested earlier in the month were released without charge by police, but immediately taken into the custody of the UK Borders Agency. One man, who had already been released, was similarly treated. The other two men remained in police custody for a further day, before being discharged, one into the custody of the Borders Agency, while the other, a British citizen, was reportedly 'staying at a hotel while police restored his home to the state it was in before extensive searches'.

Inayat Bunglawala of the Muslim Council of Britain said:

> 'It is perfectly understandable that not every arrest the police make will result in charges being brought … that is the nature of this sort of police work. What is unacceptable though is for the Government to make prejudicial remarks right at the outset. And now, now that we learn that actual evidence cannot be gathered to substantiate any terror plot, instead of releasing them with good grace and making clear a mistake has been made, the Government is seeking to deport them, citing a very vague national security threat. That is a very dishonourable way of proceeding.'

Jack Jones

As we go to press, we are sorry to receive the very sad news that Jack Jones of the Transport and General Workers' Union has died. In our next issue, we will discuss Jack's lifelong work for peace, socialism and workers' control.

GMB Campaigning against global exploitation

Making a difference
for shipbreakers and related industries in India

GMB
PROTECTING YOU AT WORK

GMB MAKING A DIFFERENCE

GMB is working with the Mumbai Port Trust Dock and General Employees Union (MPTDGEU) in India, to create better conditions for metalworkers in shipbreaking and related industries in Mumbai and Alang in India.

NO RIGHTS
The workers toil all day for the equivalent of 50 pence. Conditions are the worst you can imagine – but as the workers themselves say, 'exploitation is better than starvation'.

There is a near absence of protective clothing and workers are often forced to work barefoot. They work with corrosive chemicals, asbestos and flammable and explosive toxins which are often outlawed in the West. They operate dangerous machinery; carry heavy loads with no basic heath and safety. They are burnt, cut, bruised, blinded, there is loss of limbs, often injuries are fatal, there are no hospitals nearby and no compensation.

Home is often a mere piece of tarpaulin secured with string and stones, with no running water or access to sanitation. There are no schools, no electricity, no running water and no sanitation.

MAKING A DIFFERENCE
The MPTDGEU, formed in 1920, has a history of organising. It has already had successes in shipbreaking – providing drinkable water and creating the first shipbreakers' union. GMB is involved in developing a project which will see the unionisation and organising of metal workers in the industry, bringing an end to this brutal form of exploitation masquerading as 'globalisation'.

JOIN WITH GMB AND MAKE A DIFFERENCE
You can make a donation which will go directly to benefit the members of our sister union the MPTDGEU, or you can specifically sponsor one of the following items – large or small, everything helps.

The office of the MPTDGEU – The Workers House – is at the very heart of the community. It provides free space to a local primary school, there is a school for the children of shipbreakers, educational programmes for workers and women, health programmes, and political and social meetings take place here.

SCHOOL
A bare room with 30 children who sit on rush mats. They need everything.
- Teacher's salary (per month) **£120**
- Whiteboard, pens and duster **£12**
- Text books, standard level 1 to 4 (£12 x 30) **£360***
- Text books, standard level 5 to 10 (£15 x 30) **£450***
- Note books (per hundred) **£15**
- Ball point pens (per hundred) **£4**
- Pencils (per hundred) **£3**
- Story books **£1**
- Equipment, erasers, sharpeners, compass (per child) **£1.20**

*These books can be used for years

OLDER PEOPLE
- Medicines/operations **£10** to **£30**
- Umbrellas **£1**
- Zimmer **£8.50**
- Tricycle **£60**
- Ex gratia pension to those with no income and no person earning in the family (per month) **£18**

ANTI ASBESTOS CAMPAIGN
- 2,000 T-shirts including printing costs **£1,600**
- Banner for anti asbestos campaign **£15**
- Placards **£100**

COMMUNICATION
- Purchase of radio/megaphone **£60**
- Film projector **£720**
- Computer **£600**

RECRUITMENT OFFICER
- Sponsor a worker for a year **£2,000**

SEWING PROJECT
- Purchase of three sewing machines (each) **£300**
- Part-time tutor (per year) **£850**

MOTORCYCLE
The workplaces on Alang beach are spread over 10 kilometres of rough terrain, with no roads and no public transport. A motorcycle is vital to recruit and organise in this area. At a cost of **£700**

YES, I WANT TO MAKE A DIFFERENCE

GMB branch and region
Address
Telephone   Email
Donation
Towards
Or the general fund

Please make cheques payable to GMB/Shipbreaking and send with this form to Joni McDougall, GMB, 22/24 Worple Road, London SW19 4DD
If you would like further information on GMB's work or if you would like a speaker to address your branch meeting please contact Joni at the address above, or on 020 8971 4272 or joni.mcdougall@gmb.org.uk

Two, Three, Many Revolutions ...

On Tom Paine

Peter Linebaugh

Peter Linebaugh teaches history at the University of Toledo in Ohio. His books include The London Hanged *and* Magna Carta Manifesto, *reviewed in Spokesman 103. He also introduces* Thomas Paine *comprising* Common Sense, The Rights of Man *and* Agrarian Justice, *to be published by Verso in its Revolutions series.*

A New World, Trevor *Griffiths' new play about the life of Thomas Paine, has its world première at Shakespeare's Globe in London on 29 August, and runs till 9 October.*

President Obama quoted Tom Paine in the conclusion to his inaugural address in January, but did not name him.

After Obama named the values (honesty, hard work, courage, fair play, tolerance, loyalty, and patriotism), after he urged us to our duties and responsibilities, and to be ready to pay the price of citizenship, after invoking God, and stating that these values comprised our liberty and creed, he asked us to remember America's birth (an odd name for independence or revolution when you think about it).

Obama set the scene on Christmas Day, for believers a birthday of a saviour. But let us set aside these undertones, and get to the main story: Xmas, 1776, and George Washington's storied crossing of the Delaware river. It is the subject of the 1850 painting by Emmanuel Leutze, a German '48er, who made sure to include an African American and a woman in the crew of the boat named *Revolution*. The Delaware separates New Jersey from Pennsylvania. In New Jersey British troops of George III, King of England, were marching swiftly after the multiple defeats, a rout really, in New York. In Pennsylvania the American troops were encamped - cold, sick, hungry, their enlistment tours almost up, demoralized, defeated, and wanting to go home. These were the original 'winter soldiers' after whom were named the brave Viet vets who denounced US war crimes in 1971 Detroit.

Washington planned to surprise the mercenary troops at Trenton on the day after Christmas. It would require a crossing during a windy night through the ice floes of the river. A bold, and risky decision. President Obama says, 'At the moment when the outcome of our revolution was most in doubt, the father of our nation ordered these words be read to the people …' And he quotes Tom Paine. George Washington was the commander of the army, and later he would become president. I don't think that he was called 'father of the nation' at the time. When did this title come to be applied? What is the significance of this figure of speech and how does it relate to 'birth' in this rhetoric? I'm not sure.

Anyway, Washington did not rally the troops himself but urged his officers to read what Tom Paine had written on a drumhead, by the light of campfires, published as *The Crisis in Philadelphia* ten days earlier and available in a pamphlet the day before Christmas Eve. Obama quotes –

> 'Let it be told to the future world that in the depth of winter, when nothing but hope and virtue could survive, that the city and the country, alarmed at one common danger, came forth to meet it.'

Obama then winds up his address, paraphrasing Paine – the winter, the timeless words, the icy currents, the hope and virtue, then God's grace and God's blessing, pretty much ending up monotheistically in the same way that Paine concluded the *Crisis* paper, beginning his last paragraph with thanks to God.

This *Crisis* paper is brief. We read it aloud in class in under forty-five minutes. Most everyone already knows the beginning, 'These are the times that try men's souls'. Paine is serious about the soul. He will invoke God Almighty several times, and here in the beginning he explains heaven and hell. 'The summer soldier and the sunshine patriot will, in this crisis, shrink from the service of their country; but he that stands it now, deserves the love and thanks of man and woman.' Woman. It's just a hint, but on the day after Christmas it gets the attention of these militia men.

> 'Tyranny, like hell, is not easily conquered; yet we have this consolation with us, that the harder the conflict, the more glorious the triumph. What we obtain too cheap, we esteem to lightly: it is dearness only that gives every thing its value. Heaven knows how to put a proper price upon its goods; and it would be strange indeed if so celestial an article as FREEDOM should not be highly rated.'

Here the figure of speech is commerce, cheapness and dearness, or as we would say deflation and inflation. But it's not true – dearness does not give value, not according to the labour theory of value anyway.

The body of the essay describes the retreat in flattering terms, it makes the rout sound like the soul of orderliness. He frankly admits to the panic of the soldiers, and explains that panic is useful not only because it toughens those who survive it but it also exposes the hypocrites, the waverers, the reconcilers, the secret tories. Then Paine – and this is his brilliance – instead of denouncing tories as traitors addresses them directly, and meets each of their arguments. 'Let us reason the matter together,' he says, quoting Isaiah, like Lyndon B Johnson used to do with Martin Luther King or anyone else who rocked the boat.

Another important undertone ripples through *The Crisis* and comes to the surface at the end – the ravishment of women: General Howe, commander of the British forces, was 'ravaging' New Jersey. If further defeat befalls the Americans – and this is the concluding thought — our homes will become bawdy-houses for the Hessians and 'a future race to provide for, whose fathers were shall doubt of'. This opens the mind to another meaning of legitimacy.

Nevertheless, this is an essay in a people's war; they are words of revolution advocating the forcible overthrow of the government. This is partly why, even in 2009, two-hundred-and-twenty-three years later, President Obama will not name the man with whose words he closes his address. Some Presidents name him, Franklin Roosevelt for example, but Teddy Roosevelt called him a 'filthy little atheist'.

The soldiers crossed the river, and before marching to Trenton to surprise the Hessian mercenaries (who surrendered with scarcely a fight), they were issued fresh gunpowder and new flints for their muskets. Paine wasn't just a wordsmith; he was handy, a tinkerer, a mechanic. He experimented in gunpowder manufacturing and recommended popular mobilization of Pennsylvania kitchens for the production of saltpeter. Moreover, I think he knew something about flints.

He was born in Thetford, East Anglia, England. I visited there a while ago with a friend, a geographer, who explained the peculiarities of the ecology of the region known as Breckland, as the Brecks. The region is desolate and thinly inhabited, historically because the soil is sandy, and actually because it's militarized – firing ranges for the soldiers, and an American airbase nearby. My friend explained that tools of war had been manufactured in the Brecks for centuries, nay, for millennia. Grime's Graves is the name of the Neolithic flint mining pits and galleries located not a long walk from Thomas Paine's birthplace. The spear points, hatchets, and knives made from the flint turn up as arrow-heads do among American farmers.

The production of gunflints reached the stage of industrial take-off only during the wars against the French Revolution when more than a million a month were produced at Brandon, just up the river from Thetford along the Little Ouse. A good Brandon flint knapper could hammer out eight gunflints a minute, according to the observations of Sydney B.J. Skertchly, reporting in an 1879 volume of the *Memoirs of the Geological Survey*. In a later volume of the Survey (1891), W. Whitaker notes that the cylindrical flint forms found about Thetford produced a distinctly sonorous clinking when struck against one another. He notes in the same volume that the hand-fashioned implements found in the gravel pits of Thetford 'give us our earliest evidence of the existence of our species in England', (and, as we might add, concerning the same species, the termination of its existence, for the Anglo-American have specialized their relationship there with missiles bearing nuclear warheads.)

I thought it might provide a neat fact to say that the flints issued to the army on the eve of its victory came from that part of England where the author of the fighting words came from, both igniting revolution, but I'm afraid that the provenance of the flints in question is the source of scholarly controversy. They may have actually been the preferred French flints, honey-yellow in colour, and knapped as flakes, in contrast to the black flints of Brandon which were knapped as spalls. However, the soundings by Seymour de Lotbiniere of Brandon Hall into the three hundred volumes of the 18th century Board of Ordnance records produced a few findings which were published in the *Minnesota Archaeologist*. These make it clear that it is certainly possible that the flints came from the Brecks. In 1775, the Ordnance Board puts in its first order for flake gunflints, or 'flints of a New Construction', which possessed the design advantages of those of French manufacture. Or, the flints may have been part of the câche of 30,000 black flints seized with the fall of Fort Ticonderoga in May 1775 which, according to G.M. Trevelyan, were immediately sent to Washington.

The arcana of scholarly specialists can tease the imagination. While the evidence of lithologists, petrographers, and archaeologists has produced a wealth of evidence over the Victorian pedestrian geologists, such as Skertchly or Whitaker, it does not yet tell us, conclusively, where Washington's gunflints came from. But scholarship advances! By strict reasoning and patient investigation, including fascinating new techniques such as photographic spark array analysis, we cannot exclude the possibility that the flint deposits of the region of Thetford are evidence of a) the first existence of homo sapiens in England, or b) the permanence of the propensity in that species to military hardware. Furthermore, the evidence does not permit us to say that the flints of Paine's Brecklands were c) an essential precondition to the independence of America, or, and finally, d) necessary to the victory of the rights of man! Yet I think sparking provides us with a better analogy than parturition when it comes to the revolutionary war.

Henry Knox was there, going across the river, avoiding the floating ice, marching the nine miles to Trenton in a hailstorm, marching 'with the most profound silence'. He wrote to his wife, 'It must give sensible pleasure to every friend of the rights of man to think with how much intrepidity our people pushed the enemy and prevented their forming in the town'. Thomas Paine went on to write further papers of *The Crisis*, the last and 13th called 'Thoughts on the Peace and the Probable Advantages Thereof'. It was full of grandiose hyperbole, yet Rome was on his mind, 'Rome, once the proud mistress of the universe, was originally a band of ruffians. Plunder and rapine made her rich, and her oppression of millions made her great'. And there was Obama talking about 'greatness' again! And not a word about the rights of man. Instead it has become commonplace in 2009 to talk about the US empire. We now see the American Revolution in three: the war of independence from England, the slave revolt from the plantations, and the war of conquest against the native Americans.

So, let's get back to Tom Paine's birthday. It was on January 29, 1737. This was a significant date and a significant year and for the same reason, namely both are associated with regicide. The 30th January is the anniversary of the beheading of Charles I in 1649. In England the republicans of every stripe remembered the day, as did monarchists who called Charles a martyr. That's the day. Now this for the year. 1736 was the last time that the Calve's Head Club met. This was gathering for drinks and a feast to secretly commemorate the death of monarchy and all that it stood for.

Regicide then was never far from Paine's mind, especially around his birthday. I think that he planned for it because all his major writings were generally published at this time of year. *Common Sense* in January 1776, *The Crisis* in December as we've seen, *Rights of Man* part one in February 1791, and *Rights of Man* part two exactly a year later, *The Age of Reason* which John Brown and Mother Jones alike admired, was published in January 1794, and *Agrarian Justice,* in which he distinguished between natural and acquired property, arguing that earth, air, and water belonged to all as a commons, was published in the winter of 1795.

Though a revolutionary opposing kingship, one-man rule, the puppet-show of sovereignty, the war-making essential to monarchy, he was also opposed to capital punishment, refusing in France to vote for the execution of Louis XVI and Marie Antoinette. He was cast into prison and escaped the guillotine himself only by an amazing accident – the doors of those to be guillotined were chalked the night before, but Paine's cell door was not yet closed but swung open against the wall and in the dim light it was chalked on the wrong side, so that when closed at last it displayed the unchalked side when the executioners came in the morning.

In the nineteenth century the anniversary of the regicide, the 30th January, was no longer much observed. On the other hand, the birthday of Tom Paine, the 29th January, was the occasion for banquets, drinks, and celebrations by reformers and revolutionists such as William Lloyd Garrison, Elizabeth Cady Stanton, Susan B. Anthony, Walt Whitman, Herman Melville, Abraham Lincoln, Albert Parsons, Mark Twain, Emma Goldman, Eugene Debs, A.J. Muste, Saul Alinsky, C. Wright Mills. The list is American because I have relied on Harvey Kaye's reliable but Americentric study when America could claim to be the exceptional revolutionary beacon. About a decade later it was joined by Haiti, Ireland, France, and the hopes of many others.

'Counter-revolution', like the 'United States of America', were phrases or neologisms invented by Paine. He did not find a place for himself in post-revolutionary America, or during its counter-revolution, so he returned to England. 'From what we now see, nothing of reform on the political world ought to be held improbable. It is an age of revolutions, in which everything may be looked for.' In Ireland the United Irish were inspired by Paine's American and French experiences, which they combined in a toast of Belfast, 'May common sense establish the rights of man'. In India the Bengal renaissance of the 1840s owes much to the work of the Derozians, followers of Vivian Derozio, who taught his students at Calcutta's Hindu College both *The Rights of Man* and *The Age of Reason*. K'tut Tantri, who fought with the guerrillas and wrote speeches for Sukarno against Dutch imperialism in Indonesia, was known to her comrades as the Mrs. Tom Paine! When Paine raised his glass, in 1792, just before going over to France he toasted 'To World Revolution'.

George Lippard, co-operator, unionist, enemy of capitalists, honoured the 115th birthday of Paine: 'that unfailing quill in his hand that shall burn into the brains of kings like arrows winged with fire and pointed with vitriol'.

Ernestine Rose, a New York feminist, organized Tom Paine festivals, a birthday in 1852: 'There is no need to eulogize Thomas Paine. His life-long devotion to the cause of freedom; his undaunted, unshrinking advocacy of truth; his deep seated hatred to kingly and priestly despotism, are his best eulogies'.

Robert Ingersoll, the freethinker of Illinois, gave the Tom Paine birthday address in 1871: 'He had more brains than books; more sense than education; more courage than politeness; more strength than polish ... He saw oppression on every hand; injustice everywhere; hypocrisy at the altar; venality on the bench; tyranny on the throne; and with a splendid courage he espoused the causes of the weak against the strong – of the enslaved many against the titled few.'

Lester Ward, the Iowa reformer, in a 1912 Tom Paine birthday dinner, noted that the political struggle was not enough: 'There was another great struggle to be gone through ... a contest for the attainment of social and economic equality. It is the effort of the fourth estate which used to be called the proletariat, the working classes, the mass of mankind, to secure social emancipation.'

Mumia Abu Jamal remembers that George Washington would not lift a finger to help Paine from the guillotine, and Mumia, himself from death row, quotes Paine's bitter letter, 'And as to you, Sir, treacherous in private friendship (for so you have been to me, and that in the day of danger) and hypocrite in public life, the world will be puzzled to decide whether you are an apostate or an imposter, whether you have abandoned your principles, or whether you ever had any.' The sunshine patriot refused to aid the winter soldier, or 'the father of his country' refused to stand by ... what? the mother? the Lamaze midwife? instead leaving Thomas Paine to the dungeon and the guillotine.

Mumia sums up, 'Thoroughly radical, a believer in international revolution, an opponent of slavery, anti-death penalty, and advocate for the poor, Thomas Paine embodied some of the most humanistic movements of his time.'

Thomas Paine was fond of a certain time of year. He concludes part two of *Rights of Man* by referring to it. 'It is now towards the middle of February,' he says. 'Were I to take a turn into the country, the trees would present a leafless winterly appearance.' It is not as easy now in 2009 to take such a turn in the country because leisurely strolls have all but vanished given overall social speed-up, and the country is not what it used to be either, but is asphalted in strip malls and subdivisions. Still, perhaps we remember people taking such walks. 'As people are apt to pluck twigs as they walk along, I perhaps might do the same, and by chance might observe, that a single bud on that twig had begun to swell.' This gentle sentence is the key to Paine: notice how in the logic and the grammar of it the author follows the reader.

Furthermore, the sentence expresses the first step in reaching an accurate conclusion about the real world, the scientific method begins with the making of an observation. Then comes the second step, reasoning. 'I should reason very unnaturally, or rather not reason at all, to suppose this was the only bud in England which had this appearance. Instead of deciding thus, I should instantly conclude, that the same appearance was beginning, or about to begin, everywhere; and though the vegetable sleep will continue longer on some trees and plants than on others, and though some of them may not blossom for two or three years, all will be in leaf in the summer, except those which are rotten.' Nations and individuals are his matter. Some people can flower, i.e. learn, flourish, speak and act, some quicker than others, some not at all. Likewise, some nations can throw off despotism. 'What pace the political summer may keep with the natural, no human foresight can determine. It is, however, not difficult to perceive that the spring is begun.'

The essential point, popular sovereignty, is introduced at last as an adjective and the seasons or the summer, the turning of the earth on its axis towards the sun, is the real world of us all – 'the political summer'. And the paragraph ends with the powerful word 'spring', here as one of the seasons, and as we now think about it as one of the stages in revolutionary transformation. But spring is also a verb, a very active one, sudden, a leap. And this is what revolutionaries do – they jump and they surprise, here, there, all over. They do it together, and nowadays we must do it by commoning.

Paine's prose reflects his deep beliefs – a) the passage begins and ends not with abstract theories, or imagined romances, but with a real objective world common to us all – earth, air, water, b) the common person may understand that world by observation and reasoning, c) the change is accomplished by action. I should not say the prose reflects these beliefs, because the prose does not say these things directly. Instead, we think them as a result of the prose. Paine guides us; he helps us think. But we do the thinking. The only thing in the passage which might give us pause– it is two centuries old – is that we live in post-enclosure time, our country, our world, is enclosed, shut up. His had not yet been, or not completely. In England, 1804 was the Thetford Enclosure Act privatizing 5,616 acres and denying public access to 80 per cent of the borough.

This year is the bicentennial of the death of Thomas Paine. He died in what is now Greenwich Village and was buried in New Rochelle attended by a French woman, some Irish men, and two Afro-Americans.

Let us lift our bumpers high for Citizen Tom Paine, for spark array analysis, and world revolution.

• Note: I thank the geographer Iain Boal, I thank Gillian Boal for provision of my notebooks, I thank Alan Haber for provision of Howard Fast's edition of *Selected Writings of Thomas Paine* (1945), a book which J. Edgar Hoover ordered taken from the shelves of American public libraries, and I thank the generosity of Oliver Bone, curator at the Ancient House, Thetford, for photocopying some pages from Alan Crosby, *A History of Thetford* (1986).

SOME FURTHER READING
Harvey J. Kaye, *Thomas Paine and the Promise of America* (2005)
John Keane, *Tom Paine: A Political Life* (1995)
Henry Steel Commager and Richard B. Morris, *The Spirit of 'Seventy-Six: The Story of the American Revolution as Told by Participants* (1958)
Craig Nelson, *Thomas Paine: Enlightenment, Revolution, and the Birth of Modern Nations* (2006)
Eric Foner, *Tom Paine and Revolutionary America* (1976)
David Hackett Fisher, *Washington's Crossing* (2004)
Trevor Griffiths, *These are the Times: A Life of Thomas Paine* (2005)
Joyce Chumbley and Leo Zonneveld (editors), *Thomas Paine: In Search of the Common Good* (2009)

COMMUNICATION WORKERS UNION

May Day greetings to all readers of *The Spokesman*

Billy Hayes
General Secretary

Davie Bowman
President

Keynes and the G20 Altering the World Money

1. On Redistribution of Income

Michael Barratt Brown

Michael Barratt Brown's book Global Crisis *treats extensively the problem of redistribution of wealth (Spokesman Books, 1999, £9)*

'Speculators may do no harm as bubbles on a steady stream of enterprise. But the position is serious when enterprise becomes the bubble on the whirlpool of speculation. When the capital development of a country becomes a by-product of the activities of a casino, the job is likely to be ill done.'
John Maynard Keynes

It is said that everyone in the current crisis is a Keynesian – in believing that governments must spend their way out of a crisis rather than cutting back their spending. But it is not recognised that Keynes meant spending on job creation and especially on capital projects, not just bailing out the speculators. The argument is relatively simple, as it applied to the crisis of the 1930s, but I have not seen it being rehearsed in all the articles and correspondence concerning the current crisis. It runs as follows: Keynes distinguished a consumption sequence in the market, and an investment sequence. The first was determined by what he called 'aggregate demand' for goods, the rate of consumers' decisions to spend. The second was determined by the rate of saving for investment, mostly by those richer people and companies with capital to invest in productive activities. During boom years the proportion of incomes going to saving rose, so that there were more savings available for investment, by which Keynes meant actual purchases of capital goods. For a time capital investment rose, but, if consumption did not rise in line with this new capacity to invest in producing goods, a crisis arose. Capital investment in production was suddenly stopped as surplus stocks built up. Those with capital looked for other uses for it.

Keynes argued that there was nothing in the market model to ensure that the balance between savings and consumption was equal to the balance between investment in capital goods and the production of consumption goods. It was supposed that the rate of interest on savings would act as a regulator of the balance. But, while a high rate of interest would encourage saving, it would discourage investment; and a low rate would discourage saving, but would not necessarily encourage investment. The last would depend upon the demand for production of consumer goods. In other words, the interest rate could pull activity down, acting like a piece of string, but string cannot push things up. Keynes never said that the savers were the richer members of any society, and the consumers the poorer. That would have sounded too much like Marx's critique of Capital.

The chief doubt that Keynes had about the efficacy of lower interest rates was that when rates were low and there was little or no more demand for consumption, then most savers preferred liquidity, i.e. to hold on to their cash beyond what was needed for paying debts. This is where everything has changed since Keynes' day. He was thinking of a largely closed economy without freedom of capital movements. The change is that economic globalisation means that controls on capital movements have been eliminated, so that holders of capital – persons and institutions including the banks – who once preferred liquidity can move their funds wherever they can see a profitable move, which is frequently a speculative activity. A large proportion of the sale of derivatives takes place across international borders. The other element in globalisation is the reduction of regulation not only of capital movements, but also of risk taking in general. This is what enabled the banks to indulge in the provision of mortgages without adequate guarantees of repayment, resulting in the widespread housing crisis in the United States and the United Kingdom. Huge sums of money were earned by the speculators, while the incomes of the mass of the population stagnated. Keynes recognised that growing inequality of incomes was the basic cause of crisis. The poorer people could not consume so much; the richer could not find so much demand for their capital investment in production. In the absence of consumer demand for more goods, what the rich turned to was speculation, which Keynes did not think was a good thing, as the epigraph to this article indicates.

Keynes had noticed that when slump replaced boom, the first and heaviest falls took place in the capital investment goods sector as aggregate demand in the market for consumption goods declined. He therefore recommended governments to spend more money on the production of capital goods – houses, schools, railways, roads, energy and other parts of an economy's infrastructure. He would certainly not have given state funds to the bankers who would not necessarily invest it in new production, whether of capital goods or consumer goods, thus creating new employment. He would have given it to local government authorities and regional authorities like the Tennessee Valley Authority in the USA, for providing public and social services and construction schemes, as Roosevelt did in following Keynesian measures in his New Deal legislation to get the US out of the 1930s slump, the last deep slump before the present one.

Income inequality

Growing inequality of incomes was recognised by Professor J.K. Galbraith in his classic work, *The Great Crash 1929,* as the fundamental cause of the 1930s slump. Between 1922 and 1930 profits in US manufacturing industry rose in real terms by 130%, while real earnings rose by only 17%. Similar figures have been recorded for the US in the last decade, and the previous decade of the 1990s saw an actual fall in real wages while profits boomed. The British Government has claimed that inequality of incomes was actually reduced after New Labour took power in 1997. There was a very small reduction up to 2002 in the difference between the share of UK incomes of the top 20% and of the bottom 20%, but the gap widened again thereafter. The distribution of post-tax incomes between high, medium and low quintiles was almost exactly the same in 2007/8 as it had been ten years earlier, when New Labour came to power; and this was after Mrs Thatcher and John Major had greatly widened the inequalities. The rich had continued to become richer, especially the top few per cent of incomes, and New Labour had done nothing to increase the taxes on the rich.

The United Kingdom was not, however, the only place where inequalities had increased. The widest gap had opened up in the United States, where profits had risen steadily while wages in real terms had hardly risen over two decades. In the 1990s similar gaps had opened up elsewhere, especially in Latin America, but also in the areas of economic growth, most especially in China, but in India also. The gap between rich and poor in Russia was unparalleled. Moreover, average incomes in the Developing Countries, as a whole but particularly in Africa, were falling behind those in the Developed. This was partly due to falling prices of primary commodities relative to those of finished manufactures, when Developing Countries were still dependent on income from their commodity exports. But other reasons were even more important, associated with the privatisation of state assets.

Privatisation of public companies was begun by Pinochet in Chile, and under the Thatcher and Reagan governments in the United Kingdom and United States in the 1980s, but it became widespread in the 1990s. Russia provided the most extreme example, but the privatising process was taking place elsewhere in Europe, and most particularly in China and also in Latin America. Instead of raising taxes, which were unpopular, especially among the rich, governments were meeting the demands of public spending by selling off state assets. Two reasons were given for these sales. The first was that state enterprises were a drain on public resources. In fact, World Bank reports record that foreign borrowing was generally covering any deficits in public accounts in most Developing Countries; the second was that public enterprise was inefficient. This reason for privatisation has always been used, and still is adhered to quite religiously by British Governments. The late lamented Andrew Glyn in his major work on British capitalism, in 2006, argued that there was no evidence of improved efficiency, in productivity for example, after privatisation in the United Kingdom. Nor can the argument of harmful vested state interest stand up against similar arguments against crony capitalism. What is clear is that political pressures and not any economic rationale were driving privatisation, and in Developing Countries the main pressure was coming from the IMF and the World Bank. The neoliberal consensus had become universal, that the market should be left to allocate resources with minimal state regulation and maximum freedom for capital movements.

The changed role of the banks

This has led to a new role being taken by the banks. Instead of simply holding their customers' moneys and lending money out beyond the value of their holdings, at agreed rates of interest related to the official bank rate, in order to finance business activity, the banks had begun to conduct trading operations themselves. Much of this has been speculative, buying or borrowing company shares in order to sell them at a profit, and lending money for mortgages without guarantees that the mortgage payments could be maintained. It was, as we have seen, the latter that led to the crisis in the United States and also in the United Kingdom. The banks' buying of shares, often in very large companies, encouraging a great number of mergers and take-overs, also led to much risk taking of debt and ultimate bank failures. The development of hedge funds and private equity groups has been a particularly large element of what Peter Gowan, in a brilliant editorial in *New Left Review* (no 55 Jan/Feb 2009, pp.5-29), calls 'The

New Wall Street System' and has led to the current financial crisis. Gowan makes it clear that the City of London has not just been an adjunct of Wall Street but a major player, boasting of the most unregulated market in the world and, in 2007, having a global share of 42.5 % of derivatives. (That is to say, moneys whose value depends on the value of something else, i.e. varying forms of credit.)

What, then, should be done with the banks, to start with the British banks? Just bailing them out hasn't worked and cannot be made to work with the banks' accumulated mass of mortgage and other debt. Money will have to be made available by government to help those in danger of dispossession of their homes, but not once more in the hands of the commercial banks. There is an obvious alternative, which would have popular support – the Post Office. Closing it down as was originally intended by Lord Mandelson, to have some of its functions replaced by the giant retail companies, was no solution. Mandelson has now apparently recognised that the Post Office Bank needs to be brought into action as an agent of public sector finance, starting with houses and going on to providing credit for small businesses. This must be a good move if the commercial banks can be left to return to their original role. Their shareholders and chief executives could then be made to suffer; it was they who got us into the mess we are in. A distinction must be made among the banks. Some like the Co-op Bank and Nationwide and some other Building Societies are mutual associations, which do not have shareholders, receiving a dividend; all members are owners. Many mutuals went private in the last two decades, which looks like a mistake because it is a significant fact that those that remained mutuals have not engaged in the risky investments of the private banks and have not suffered the same failures. Nor for that matter has the Post Office Bank.

Next steps

The international monetary authorities have rightly judged that the United Kingdom will have the greatest difficulty of all states in recovering from the current crisis, and this for three reasons. The first is the scale of the house mortgage debt; the second is the extent of British commercial banks' involvement in hedging and trade in derivatives; the third is the failure of government fiscal policy, to build up a surplus in the good years to be available when things went bad. The first two can only be dealt with by abandoning the commercial banks so that they cannot repeat past errors and, as already suggested, by reactivating the Post Office Bank with heavy state support. The third problem of the government deficit can be overcome by taking ruthless steps to retrieve the vast sums that the rich have squirreled away in tax havens in British territories, chiefly the Isle of Man, the Channel Islands, Cayman Islands and the Bahamas. Before becoming Chancellor, Gordon Brown promised to address this leaking of funds, but in fact it grew steadily year by year under his chancellorship, to a figure quoted even by the Government Department of Customs and Revenue as amounting to over £13 billion. Other estimates are much higher, at twice that figure.

What remains to be decided is how to spend the resources available to government so as to increase employment and offset the increasing loss of confidence in the British economy, and especially what not to spend money on. The first and most obvious step is to end the useless and dangerous military expenditure in pursuing the wars in Iraq and Afghanistan and replacing Trident. Government expenditure which encourages road and air travel could be cut, but there is a positive alternative. A great window of opportunity opens up for combining recovery with essential steps to stave off the disastrous effects of our wasteful carbon emissions, contributing greatly to what is euphemistically called 'climate change', but is in effect a climate disaster already overwhelming the planet . A massive programme of house insulation and adaptation needs to be launched, combined with projects for developing sources of energy from wind, solar and wave power. All such activities would be highly effective in generating new employment and business confidence. The agents for managing these programmes and their owners should be local and regional authorities and specially created and designated public bodies. The success of Roosevelt's Tennessee Valley Authority is already being recalled by President Obama. Management of recovery should not be through what is quite absurdly proposed by Gordon Brown – the extension of Private Finance Initiatives. These have been failing in recent months and depend on commercial bank credit, which thanks to bank failures is just what is not now available.

If Gordon Brown and Alastair Darling fail to end the 'New Wall Street System' in Britain and set sail on a new course, it seems possible that the Tories might do it. Philip Blond, director of the Progressive Conservatism Project at the DEMOS think-tank, has already in an article in *Prospect* (February 2009, pp.32-36) proposed some of the measures that have been suggested above, including a revamped Post Office Bank. This may have been what persuaded Lord Mandelson to change his mind about the Post Office. What is for sure is that Mandelson and Brown have to be held to their promises. There must be a real ban on the rich salting their money away in tax havens, and the Post Office Bank must be given the resources to be a major agent of the Government's recovery programme. None of this will happen without a groundswell of support for alternative policies to end the bankers' ramp. Massive demonstrations in France and near civil war in Greece have begun to be echoed by the strike of construction and power workers in England, with sympathy actions elsewhere, especially in Wales and Scotland. At some point, anger will have to be turned into positive action.

Ditch the Dollar

A UN panel will recommend that the world ditch the dollar as its reserve currency in favour of a shared basket of currencies, a member of the panel has said. Avinash Persaud, one of the Commission of Experts on International Financial Reform, said in Luxemburg that the proposal was to create something like the old Ecu, or European currency unit. 'There is a moment that can be grasped for change,' he said. 'Today the Americans complain that when the world wants to save, it means a deficit. A shared (reserve) would reduce the possibility of global imbalances.'

Persaud said the UN panel had been looking at using something like an expanded Special Drawing Right, originally created by the International Monetary Fund in 1969. The SDR and the old Ecu are essentially combinations of currencies, weighted to a constituent's economic clout, which can be valued against other currencies and indeed against those inside the basket.

Persaud said there were two main reasons why policymakers might consider such a move, one being the current desire for a change from the dollar. The other reason, he said, was the success of the euro, which incorporated a number of currencies but roughly speaking held on to the stability of the old German deutschemark compared with, say, the Greek drachma.

Persaud has long argued that the dollar would give way to the Chinese yuan as a global reserve currency within decades. A shared reserve currency might negate this move, he said, but he believed that China would still like to take on the role.

Source: Reuters, 18 March 2009

2. On Bretton Woods

Stuart Holland

We reprint this excerpt from Stuart Holland's book Towards a New Bretton Woods: Alternatives for the Global Economy *(Spokesman Books, 1994).*

Keynes' major contribution in *The General Theory*[1] in 1936 had been on the demand side of national economic policy. As he put it in his *Concluding Notes* [chapter 24]:

> provided the state intervened to manage the level of demand, the processes of perfect and imperfect competition would by and large take care of what was produced, in what way and on what scale, as well as 'how the value of the final product would be distributed'.

The contribution of Keynes at Bretton Woods reflected his reasoning in a paper which had been published in April 1943, and whose plan was the following.

We need an instrument of international currency having general acceptability between nations, so that blocked balances and bilateral clearings are unnecessary ...

We need an orderly and agreed method of determining the relative exchange values of national currency units, so that unilateral action and competitive exchange depreciations are prevented.

We need a quantum of international currency, which is neither determined in an unpredictable and irrelevant manner as, for example, by the technical progress of the gold industry, nor subject to large variations depending on the gold reserve policies of individual countries; but is governed by the actual current requirements of world commerce, and is also capable of deliberate expansion and contraction to offset deflationary and inflationary tendencies in effective world demand.

We need a system possessed of an internal stabilising mechanism by which pressure is exercised on any country whose balance of payments with the rest of the world is departing from equilibrium in either direction, so as to prevent movements which must create for its neighbours an equal but opposite want of balance.

We need an agreed plan for starting off every country after the war with a stock of reserves appropriate to its importance in world commerce, so that without undue anxiety it can set its house in order during the transitional period to full peace-time conditions.

We need a central institution, of a purely technical and non-political character, to aid and support other international institutions concerned with the planning and regulation of the world's economic life.

More generally, we need a means of reassurance to a troubled world, by which any country whose own affairs are conducted with due prudence is relieved of anxiety for causes which are not of its own making, concerning its ability to meet its international liabilities; and which will, therefore, make unnecessary those methods of restriction and discrimination which countries have adopted hitherto, not on their merits, but as measures of self-protection from disruptive outside forces.

Bretton Woods and after

The establishment of the International Monetary Fund *(IMF)* and the International Bank for Reconstruction and Development (the World Bank) was influenced by Keynes, but in practice dominated by the United States and its prevailing economic orthodoxies. Both institutions were the outcome of the conference at Bretton Woods in New Hampshire in 1944 to agree on a system of international payments for the post-war period, and which included representatives of the key countries that had taken part in the alliance against Germany, Italy and Japan.

Keynes himself later said that the International Monetary Fund ought to be called a bank and the World Bank should be called a fund. This name game was to be reflected in a constrained role for the World Bank in the later post-war period. In terms of the Bretton Woods objectives, the IMF was supposed to deal with short-term foreign-exchange and balance-of-payments problems. The World Bank was scheduled not for project finance but for the more ambitious aim of global development.

On the trade and payments front, Keynes was concerned that the key lessons should be learned from the crises of the 1930s. In his view, a system of floating exchange rates could lead to disaster in international economic affairs.

One of the vital roles of the Fund in what might be called the 'post Keynesian' period of its operation, was to achieve an ordered system for exchange-rate changes. It was anticipated that such changes would be made only in the face of serious and persistent disequilibria in the balance of payments of individual countries, and only after consultation with the IMF. IMF lending to an individual country would be conditional on evaluation of the viability of a particular exchange rate.

By contrast with this short-term interventionist role anticipated for the IMF, the International Bank for Reconstruction and Development, or World Bank, was designed to facilitate long-term capital movements. With funds of its own, the Bank can in principle lend to countries in need for development purposes – but also like the IMF – its lending gives 'a seal of approval' which legitimates additional private bank spending in such countries.

In practice – and contrary to widespread public perception – Keynes did not in fact gain his basis for a new international economic order at Bretton Woods. Sir Roy Harrod[2] has chronicled Keynes' exchanges with his formal antagonist at the conference – US representative Harry White. But Keynes' real antagonist was the profound conservatism of a US establishment much less convinced than an already ailing President Roosevelt that the Bretton Woods system would establish a global New Deal.

Keynes had been ambitious for the IMF. He wanted it to overcome the preoccupation with available savings to finance investment, and instead provide sufficient finance to meet increased demand with increased investment and output. The issue as to whether one has the money today to finance investment or whether one should create credit instruments to increase investment, jobs and income has been one of the ongoing differences between Keynesians and monetarists through the 1970s and 1980s.

Such analytic differences about the role of public borrowing became subsumed at Bretton Woods into how big the new IMF's lending facilities should be. Keynes envisaged an IMF scheme involving funds some *five times* those advocated by White. In practice the final act of Bretton Woods contained a compromise figure much closer to the White recommendations than to those of Keynes. As Harrod (1963, p.549) stressed:

> Keynes wanted a fund so large as to give governments the confidence necessary to relax unneighbourly restriction; $25 billion might have achieved that (the Keynes plan); $5 billion (the White plan) certainly would not. Was this Fund really to be the foundation for the building of a better world? Or was it to be merely a modest subscription towards meeting some of the needs of poorer countries? Contemporary and subsequent opinions outside the United States have on the whole agreed in holding that Keynes was right.

One could only console oneself by hoping that, should the Americans prove obdurate now, the Fund might be enlarged in the course of its operation.

Allowing for the facility introduced since the late 1970s (whereby central banks can exchange unwanted dollars for Special Drawing Rights or SDRs), Keynes' proposals for IMF quotas, translated into current terms, could have meant a level of official quotas equivalent to between a fifth and a quarter of current trade. As it is, the leading industrial economies at the end of 1984 had reserves excluding gold equal to only the value of some two months' import trade, while the ratio of such reserves to import finance for all the market economies was only some 10 weeks.

The marginal role of the World Bank can be illustrated by the fact that, by 1985, disbursed resources were equivalent to less than two per cent of global debt. Meanwhile, as illustrated in Figure 1, the IMF quotas which Keynes intended should offset temporary payments deficits and avoid domestic deflation had shrunk from an eighth to less than a twentieth of world import trade between 1950 and 1975, i.e. at the time when they were needed to provide an alternative to the devalued dollar and to beggar-my-neighbour deflation by the OECD countries.

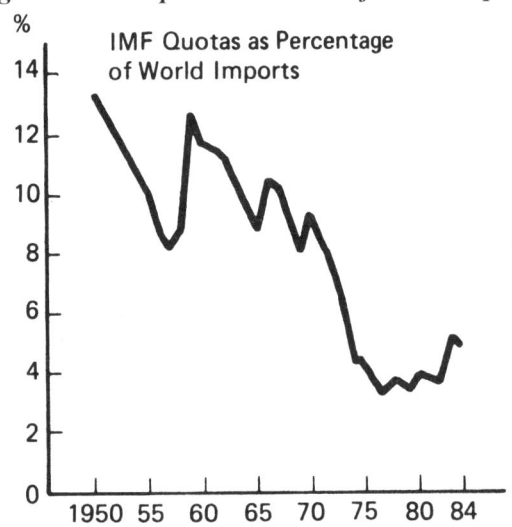

Figure 1: IMF quotas as share of world imports[3]

Bancor versus dollar dominance

Keynes wanted to see potential world demand matched by an expanding international currency unit which would not need to be fully backed either by gold or national currencies: *Bancor*. But, in reality, international trade and payments in the post-war period up to the early 1970s was dominated by the United States dollar. So long as the dollar was strong and stable, it played a primary global role, while the IMF and World Bank were upstaged minor actors. But within a quarter of a century of the Bretton Woods settlement, with its much weakened version of Keynes' own proposals, the dollar itself was under major pressure.

One of the main reasons was the recovery of Europe and Japan and the decline of US dominance. Thus while the United States in 1950 had accounted for more than half of the output of what now are the OECD countries, by 1973 this had declined to less than two-fifths.[4] The US share of world trade including the centrally planned economies had declined from about 17 per cent to 12 per cent over the same period. More strikingly, US gold reserves had fallen from nearly 70 per cent to under 30 per cent of the world total from 1950 to 1973, and to less than a quarter by 1984.

Moreover, the new post-war competitors to the United States – most notably West Germany and Japan – had managed to achieve levels of innovation, productivity and competitiveness which had already pushed the US government onto the trade defensive by the mid 1960s.

Throughout the post-war period, the United States allowed or encouraged the export of capital and direct investment on a global scale. But this tended to substitute direct foreign production for export trade, and considerably undermined US visible export performance. The emerging US dollar deficit gave rise to a market for dollars mainly managed in Europe, and soon identified as the 'Eurodollar' market, lying outside the control of the US Treasury. Meanwhile, the US trade deficit, aggravated by the Vietnam War, resulted in major pressure on the dollar and its devaluation under the Nixon administration in 1971.

Had Keynes been able to create a genuinely international reserve currency such is Bancor, the devaluation of the dollar might not of itself have resulted in the collapse of the exchange rate framework of the original Bretton Woods system. But dollar devaluation meant a significant decrease in the value of (dollar-denominated) revenues for the petroleum-producing countries, which anyway had suffered a decline in the real value of their dollar earnings per barrel of oil in preceding years. They hit back by forming OPEC. In response, as already indicated, the developed countries cut civilian public expenditure.

Such 'beggar-my-neighbour' deflation was aggravated by the re-emergence of the pre-Keynesian orthodoxy of 'sound money supply', validated in the eyes of many treasuries, chancelleries and central banks by the work of Milton Friedman and his associates. Thus, although Keynes had never wanted the dollar to be the last resort and the lynchpin of the international monetary system, combined with inflationary tendencies from the mid 1960s, this represented a profound challenge to the viability of so-called Keynesian policies in the international economy.

Footnotes
1. Keynes, J.M., (1936) *The General Theory of Employment. Interest and Money,* Macmillan. London.
2. Harrod, R.F., *The Life of John Maynard Keynes,* Macmillan, London, 1963.
3. Source: IMF and *The Economist*.
4. The increase in the US share of OECD output by 1984 reflected both the sustained expansion of the American economy and the restraint on growth in the other principal OECD economies. In contrast with the low share of the US in world total exports in 1984, US imports were 19 per cent of the world total, reflecting the vast trade deficit which accompanied the US 'boom'.

3. Unfinished business

Ken Coates

As if to offset the dismal reports from various battlefronts, the summit of the G20 has been welcomed as a breakthrough in international co-operation. But thoughtful commentators are now telling us to focus not on the G20 nations, but the G2. The G2 are the United States and China, and their accord is required if the agreement of the G20 to treble the funds available to the International Monetary Fund is to become a reality. The G20 thought it was necessary to multiply IMF resources to $750 billion, and also to sustain a $250 billion allocation of Special Drawing Rights (SDRs), which would enable the IMF to go some way towards meeting the innumerable demands which are about to be made on it. But all this extra money has to be gathered in, and if it is to be made available, then the rules of the IMF will require serious attention. This takes us back to the origins of the organisation.

Lord Keynes had proposed that the IMF should float a new currency unit of account, the Bancor. Fierce and sustained opposition from the Americans put a stop to this heresy, and anchored the post-war world to institutions which depended on the dollar. Now the Chinese have expressed their concerns about the reliability of the dollar, and floated the idea of a 'super-sovereign reserve currency'. Clearly the Chinese intend to claim the honours for reviving the unalloyed wisdom of J. M. Keynes.

Whatever the truth of this matter, it remains at first blush unlikely that the Americans are going to meet the raising of this ghost with any enthusiasm. Over the decades they have threatened to die in the last ditch to prevent the rebirth of pure Keynesianism, and there is little evidence

Ken Coates is editor of The Spokesman.

that this response will not continue. But these are difficult times, and China's weight is getting ever heavier ...

What is plain is that the institutions of the IMF will not be easy to rescue unless they are modified. Chinese resources will require Chinese influence, in considerable measure. If this does not happen then the joyful announcements about the impending Chinese rescue of the IMF may prove premature.

Zhou Xiaochuan, who is the governor of the People's Bank of China, has proposed measures to enhance the global role of Special Drawing Rights, amounting to a sweeping reform of the international monetary system. Mr. Zhou has received strong support from other Asian countries, and significantly from Brazil and Russia. But up to now, the United States has rejected the new proposals, and warned that they could undermine confidence in the dollar. However, the dollar is already weakened, and Chinese Premier Wen registered this weakness when he called for guarantees that China's vast dollar holdings would not be undermined.

Mr. Zhou's proposals would create open-ended Special Drawing Rights, which could be underpinned by the tottering dollar balances. Instead of converting the dollars, in which they were losing faith, through normal market channels, these dollars would be deposited in an IMF account for Special Drawing Rights. These would be liquid assets paying a market rate of return, and offering the necessary measures of diversification, since the SDR is denominated against a basket of currencies (44% Dollars, 34% Euros and 11% each of Yen and Sterling).

By these means, dollar holders would be offered prompt diversification, and avoid a freefall of the value of their holdings. Europe would be insured against destabilising rises in the Euro and a potential instability would be checked. The price for the Chinese would be substantial contributions to the new lending facilities, but Americans and Europeans would have to agree to a major rise in Chinese voting rights at the IMF. Historically the Europeans have been over-represented in that forum, but if there were to be a solid agreement between China and America, such a rebalancing of IMF decision-making could become irreversible.

The post-war political settlement, following 1945, endured on the political plane until 1989 and the rapid collapse of the Soviet Union and its alliances. The constitutional settlement still totters on, in the institutions of the United Nations. But the post-war economic settlement underwent a more ragged evolution. Today the reckoning looks more complex, and more disadvantageous to the powers in the West than ever seemed likely before. Revisions in the role of the IMF may be painful to negotiate, but these are going to be interesting times.

4. How to do it

Zhou Xiaochuan

The outbreak of the current crisis and its spillover in the world have confronted us with a long-existing but still unanswered question: what kind of international reserve currency do we need to secure global financial stability and facilitate world economic growth, which was one of the purposes for establishing the IMF? There were various institutional arrangements in an attempt to find a solution, including the Silver Standard, the Gold Standard, the Gold Exchange Standard, and the Bretton Woods system. The above question, however, as the ongoing financial crisis demonstrates, is far from being solved. It has become even more severe due to the inherent weaknesses of the current international monetary system.

Theoretically, an international reserve currency should first be anchored to a stable benchmark, and issued according to a clear set of rules, therefore to ensure orderly supply; second, its supply should be flexible enough to allow timely adjustment according to changing demand; third, such adjustments should be disconnected from economic conditions and sovereign interests of any single country. The acceptance of credit-based national currencies as major international reserve currencies, as is the case of the current system, is a rare special case in history. The crisis again calls for creative reform of the existing international monetary system towards an international reserve currency with a stable value, rule-based issuance, and manageable supply, so as to achieve the objective of safeguarding global economic and financial stability.

Zhou Xiaochuan is the Governor of the People's Bank of China.

I

The outbreak of the crisis and its spillover to the entire world reflect the inherent vulnerabilities and systemic risks in the existing international monetary system.

Issuing countries of reserve currencies are constantly confronted with the dilemma between achieving their domestic monetary policy goals and meeting other countries' demand for reserve currencies. On the one hand, the monetary authorities cannot simply focus on domestic goals without carrying out their international responsibilities. On the other hand, they cannot pursue different domestic and international objectives at the same time. They may either fail to adequately meet the demand of a growing global economy for liquidity as they try to ease inflation pressures at home, or create excess liquidity in the global markets by overly stimulating domestic demand. The Triffin Dilemma still exists: countries that issue reserve currencies cannot maintain the value of those reserve currencies while providing liquidity to the world.

When a national currency is used to price primary commodities, in trade settlements, and is adopted as a reserve currency globally, efforts of the monetary authority issuing such a currency to address its economic imbalances by adjusting the exchange rate would be made in vain, as its currency serves as a benchmark for many other currencies. While benefiting from a widely accepted reserve currency, globalization also suffers from the flaws of such a system. The frequency and increasing intensity of financial crises following the collapse of the Bretton Woods system suggests the costs of such a system to the world may have exceeded its benefits. The price is becoming increasingly higher, not only for the users, but also for the issuers of the reserve currencies. Although crisis may not necessarily be an intended result of the issuing authorities, it is an inevitable outcome of the institutional flaws.

II

The desirable goal of reforming the international monetary system, therefore, is to create an international reserve currency that is disconnected from individual nations, and is able to remain stable in the long run, thus removing the inherent deficiencies caused by using credit-based national currencies.

Though the super-sovereign reserve currency has long since been proposed, no substantive progress has been achieved to date. Back in the 1940s, Keynes had already proposed to introduce an international currency unit named 'Bancor', based on the value of 30 representative commodities.

Unfortunately, the proposal was not accepted. The collapse of the Bretton Woods system, which was based on the White approach, indicates that the Keynesian approach may have been more far-sighted. The IMF also created Special Drawing Rights (SDRs) in 1969, when the defects of the Bretton Woods system initially emerged, to mitigate the inherent risks sovereign reserve currencies caused. Yet, the role of the Special Drawing Rights has not been fully put into play due to limitations on its allocation and the scope of its uses. However, it serves as the light in the tunnel for the reform of the international monetary system.

A super-sovereign reserve currency not only eliminates the inherent risks of credit-based sovereign currency, but also makes it possible to manage global liquidity. A super-sovereign reserve currency managed by a global institution could be used to both create and control global liquidity. And when a country's currency is no longer used as the yardstick for global trade, and as the benchmark for other currencies, the exchange rate policy of the country would be far more effective in adjusting economic imbalances. This will significantly reduce the risks of a future crisis and enhance crisis management capability.

III

The reform should be guided by a grand vision and begin with specific deliverables. It should be a gradual process that yields win-win results for all

The re-establishment of a new and widely accepted reserve currency, with a stable valuation benchmark, may take a long time. The creation of an international currency unit, based on the Keynesian proposal, is a bold initiative that requires extraordinary political vision and courage. In the short run, the international community, particularly the IMF, should at least recognize and face up to the risks resulting from the existing system, conduct regular monitoring and assessment, and issue timely early warnings.

Special consideration should be shown to giving Special Drawing Rights a greater role. The SDRs have the features and potential to act as a super sovereign reserve currency. Moreover, an increase in SDR allocation would help the Fund address its resources problem, and difficulties in the voice and representation reform. Therefore, efforts should be made to push forward an SDR allocation. This will require political co-operation among member countries. Specifically, the Fourth Amendment to the Articles of Agreement and relevant resolution on SDR allocation proposed in 1997 should be approved as soon as possible so that members who joined the

Fund after 1981 could also share the benefits of the Special Drawing Rights. On this basis, consideration could be given to further increase in SDR allocation.

The scope for using Special Drawing Rights should be broadened so as to enable it to fully satisfy member countries' demand for a reserve currency.

A settlement system should be set up between Special Drawing Rights and other currencies. Therefore, the SDR, which is now only used between governments and international institutions, could become a widely accepted means of payment in international trade and financial transactions.

The use of Special Drawing Rights in international trade, commodities pricing, investment and corporate book-keeping should be actively promoted. This will help enhance the role of the SDRs, and will effectively reduce fluctuations in prices of assets denominated in national currencies and related risks.

Financial assets denominated in Special Drawing Rights should be created to increase their appeal. The introduction of SDR-denominated securities, which is being studied by the IMF, will be a good start.

Further improve the valuation and allocation of Special Drawing Rights: the basket of currencies forming the basis of SDR valuation should be expanded to include currencies of all major economies, and gross domestic product may also be included as a weight. The allocation of Special Drawing Rights can be shifted from a purely calculation-based system to a system backed by real assets, such as a reserve pool, to further boost market confidence in its value.

IV

Entrusting part of member countries' reserves to the centralized management of the International Monetary Fund will not only enhance the international community's ability to address the crisis, and maintain the stability of the international monetary and financial system, but also significantly strengthen the role of Special Drawing Rights.

Compared with separate management of reserves by individual countries, the centralized management of part of the global reserve by a trustworthy international institution, with a reasonable return to encourage participation, will be more effective in deterring speculation and stabilizing financial markets. The participating countries can also save some reserves for domestic development and economic growth. With its universal membership, its unique mandate of maintaining monetary and financial stability, and as an international 'supervisor' of the macroeconomic policies of its member countries, the International Monetary Fund, equipped with its expertise, is endowed with a natural advantage to act as the manager of its member countries' reserves.

The centralized management of its member countries' reserves by the Fund will be an effective measure to promote a greater role for the Special Drawing Rights as a reserve currency. To achieve this, the IMF can set up an open-ended SDR-denominated fund based on market practice, allowing subscription and redemption in the existing reserve currencies by various investors as desired. This arrangement will not only promote the development of SDR-denominated assets, but will also partially allow management of liquidity in the form of the existing reserve currencies. It can even lay a foundation for increasing SDR allocation to gradually replace existing reserve currencies with Special Drawing Rights.

Unite - London & Eastern Region

Woodberry
218 Green Lanes
London
N4 2HB

www.unitetheunion.org.uk

End the aggression in Gaza

Justice for the Palestinians

Solidarity with the PGFTU

Steve Hart – Regional Secretary   *Jim Kelly - Regional Chair*

Apartheid in Palestine

John Dugard

Professor Dugard is former UN Special Rapporteur on Human Rights in the Occupied Palestinian Territory, and Visiting Distinguished Professor of Law at Duke University in the United States. He gave a speech on 'Apartheid and Occupation under International Law' in March 2009, from which these excerpts are taken.

The Palestinian territory is clearly occupied territory. There's no question about this as far as the international community is concerned in respect to the West Bank. Israel has argued that, since 2005, when it withdrew its settlers and its military force from Gaza itself, that it has ceased to be an occupied territory. But the International Committee of the Red Cross and, I think, the whole of the international community, with the possible exception of the United States, reject this argument. They take the view that Gaza is effectively occupied by Israel because Israel has control of its land borders, its sea space, its air space and it conducts military incursions fairly regularly into the territory.

I think the United States' position, announced by [former US Secretary of State] Condoleezza Rice, was that it was a quite hostile entity. One doesn't quite know what that means. But one hopes that the [US President Barack] Obama administration will make it clear that it regards Gaza and the West Bank as occupied territory. Military occupation is a regime that is tolerated by international law. It's not approved. In terms of the Fourth Geneva Convention, which regulates the conduct of the occupying power, the occupying power is obliged to care for the welfare of the occupied people and, in particular, to ensure that medical facilities and educational facilities are respected and fostered. But, of course, we all know that Israel just ignores this obligation because in Palestine the international donor community is largely responsible for the welfare of the Palestinian people. It's quite clear that international law does not contemplate a lengthy period of occupation, a prolonged occupation in this case running to more than 40 years. The Israeli government tends to take the view that the longer the occupation, the less the obligations. But I think the generally accepted view is that the exact opposite applies. So, Israel is in occupation. But over the past 40 years, we've seen the addition of two other elements. That is colonialism and apartheid. And this tends to aggravate the status of the Palestinian territory.

I don't think there's any question about colonialism in the Palestinian territory, particularly in the West Bank since settlers withdrew from Gaza in 2005. We have nearly half a million Jewish settlers in the West Bank. This number is growing despite promises by successive Israeli governments that they will stop settlements. It's interesting that constructions are taking place in some 88 of the 149 settlements in the West Bank. The growth rate in the settlements is 4.5 per cent compared with 1.5 per cent in Israel itself.

It's important not only to look at settlements but also at territory in the West Bank that is set aside for military purposes and as nature reserves. Someone can say that roughly 38 percent of the West Bank is off limits to Palestinians. So, there is a form of colonialism in the West Bank, and colonialism is not tolerated by international law. It's clearly unlawful. Not only do settlements constitute a form of colonialism, they also violate the Geneva Convention. So, that's a clear illegality on the part of Israel.

The other element that has been introduced is that of apartheid. It's important to stress that apartheid is not only illegal in South Africa itself, but it's also been declared to be unlawful in international law. In 1973, there was a Convention on Apartheid adopted by the United Nations. Briefly, this Convention provides against the infliction on members of a racial group of serious bodily or mental harm, inhumane or degrading treatment, the deliberate creation of conditions preventing the full development of a racial group, and so on, by denying to such a group basic human rights and freedoms when such acts are committed for the purpose of establishing and maintaining domination by one racial group of persons over any other racial group of persons and systematically oppressing them. So, there is a general definition of apartheid. This definition has now been transferred to the Rome Statute of the International Criminal Court, and the crime of apartheid is seen as a species of crime against humanity. So, it's quite clear that apartheid is unlawful under international law.

Israel, of course, argues that its policies do not constitute apartheid. It claims that there's no racial discrimination in its practices or policies. It argues that the purpose of its occupation is simply to maintain law and order pending a peace settlement. It's not to maintain domination of one group over another. I think it's important to stress that there are major differences between apartheid as it was applied in South Africa and the policies and practices in the Palestinian occupied territories. The systems are clearly not identical. But there are many similar features. I would just like to speak about what I regard as the three dominant features of apartheid in South Africa, and examine the extent to which they apply in the Palestinian territory.

First of all, there was what was known as 'grand apartheid'; that was territorial separation. Then, there was what was incorrectly described as 'petty apartheid', which was racial discrimination. And then, thirdly, there were the security laws. How does Israel feature in respect of 'grand apartheid'? Are there Bantustans in the West Bank? I think the answer to this question is 'yes'. We do see territorial fragmentation of the kind that the South African government promoted in terms of its Bantustan policy. We see, first of all, a very clear separation being made between the West Bank and Gaza. But within the West Bank itself, we see a separation to essentially three or more territories and some additional enclaves with a centre, north and south. And it's quite clear that the Israeli government would like to see the Palestinian Authority as a kind of Bantustan puppet regime. So, there are similarities of that kind.

Then one comes to so-called 'petty apartheid' – discrimination. There's abundant evidence of such discrimination. There are, of course, separate roads for settlers and for Palestinians. And let me hasten to add that in South Africa we never had separate roads for black and white. There's the discrimination in the Seam Zone. That is the area between the Green Line and the Wall. Israeli nationals are free to enter the Seam Zone, but Palestinians require permits and they are seldom granted permits. Then, there's the whole question of building rights. As you know, under Israeli law, houses may not be built by Palestinians in East Jerusalem or in Area C of the West Bank – and that constitutes most of the West Bank – without permits. Permits are not granted in most cases, an overwhelming majority of cases, with the result that there's tremendous demolition of houses for so-called administrative reasons. We see that happening at present in Jerusalem. So, there is a housing demolition practice policy, which is also similar to that which occurred in South Africa.

Fourthly, there is freedom of movement. In South Africa, we had a pass law system which required all blacks to carry documents and to justify their existence wherever they happened to be. They were prevented from entering urban areas without special permission. Serious restrictions were placed on freedom of movement. But I think it's true to say that even more serious restrictions are imposed upon Palestinians. We have over 600 checkpoints within the West Bank itself. It's rather strange that Israel argues that it has built a so-called security barrier to keep suicide bombers out of Israel, but then, in addition, it erects these checkpoints. I tend to take the view that the sole purpose of the checkpoints is to discriminate and to humiliate.

Fifthly, there's the subject of family reunification. Again, this is a blatantly discriminatory practice. As you know, Palestinians living in Israel are not allowed to bring their spouses to Israel if they are from the Occupied Palestinian Territory, and Palestinians in the Occupied Palestinian Territory are not allowed to bring in foreign spouses either. So, we do have a discriminatory system.

Another feature of apartheid was its security apparatus. In order to maintain white control, the South African authorities introduced draconian security laws, which resulted in the detention and prosecution of a large number of political activists. But, of course, the same thing happens in Israel. We now have some 11,000 Palestinian prisoners in Israeli jails. There are very serious allegations of torture of detainees and prisoners. So what is the major difference?

The major difference I see between South Africa's apartheid system and what prevails in the Occupied Palestinian Territory is that the South African apartheid regime was more honest. We had a rigid legal system which prescribed in great detail how discrimination was to occur and how it was to be implemented. There was an obsession with detail and legality in much the same way that Nazi Germany discriminated. It was open but, at the same time, it was honest. In the case of Israel, it is concealed. There's a lovely story told by Shulamit Aloni, a former Minister of Education in Israel, of an occasion in which she confronted a member of the Israeli Defence Force who was arresting a Palestinian for driving on a settler road and confiscating his identification card. She said to him, 'But how is he to know that this is a road for the exclusive use of settlers? There is no notice to that effect.' And the soldier said, 'Of course Palestinians know or they should know.' He said, 'What do you want us to do? Do you want us to put up signs saying Palestinians only, settlers only, and then everyone will say that we are an apartheid state like South Africa?' There is this concealment of discrimination.

So, there are differences. I suppose you're going to ask me the question, which regime was worse? I find it difficult to answer this question as a white South African because, although I lived in South Africa throughout the apartheid period, I was obviously not subject to the discriminatory laws that were levelled and aimed at blacks. But what is interesting is that every black South African to whom I've spoken who has visited the Palestinian territory has been horrified, and has said without hesitation that the system that applies in Palestine is worse. There are a number of reasons for this. I think, first of all, one can say there are features of the Israeli regime in the Occupied Territory that were unknown to South Africans. We never had a wall separating black and white. I know it's called the apartheid wall, but that's really a misnomer because there was no wall of that kind in South Africa. As I've said, there were no separate roads. These are novel features of Israel's apartheid regime.

The enforcement of the regime is much stricter. We have repeated military incursions into the West Bank, let alone Gaza. Gaza tends to attract most of the attention, but there are regular raids carried out by the Israeli Defence Force into the West Bank, arrests are made, and Palestinians are shot and killed. What is interesting is that in South Africa political activists were tried by the regular criminal courts of the land in open proceedings. Whereas in Israel, Palestinians are tried by military courts, which have emergency rules and regulations inherited from the British, but they are not proper courts.

I think perhaps the most important distinguishing feature is that there are no positive features about Israel's apartheid. The South African apartheid regime did attempt to pacify the black majority by providing it with material benefits. Schools were built; universities were built; hospitals and clinics were built by the apartheid regime. Special factories were built in the black areas in order to encourage workers to work in the African areas. So, there was a very positive side, although it was a materialistic side, to the apartheid order. Whereas in the case of Israel's apartheid, Israel makes virtually no contribution to the welfare of the Palestinian people. It leaves it all to the donor community.

Of course, this also raises the question, which is debated vigorously in Palestine, about whether it is wise for the donor community to bail out Israel. Whether it would not be wiser just to withdraw and let the whole world see how nasty the Israelis are in Palestine. But that's a separate question.

Let me conclude by making some comments on the response of the international community because this is another area of great difference. You'll recall that the apartheid regime was vilified internationally in the United States, in the West and throughout the world. States subjected the apartheid regime to sanctions. The United Nations was active. It also imposed limited sanctions on South Africa. The international community took the view that apartheid was an illegal regime and everything should be done to get rid of it.

Whereas we know that in the case of Israel, although there are serious and manifest violations of international law, no action is taken by western states or by the international community. We all know the reason. I might suppose in the United States you would say ultimately the strength of the American Israel Public Affairs Committee (AIPAC) and the evangelical lobby, but I think, in the West, generally it's feelings of Holocaust guilt, as if the Palestinians were responsible for the Holocaust rather than the Europeans. We see a double standard being applied in respect of Israel. I think this has serious implications for the future. One can understand the comments made by [Sudanese] President [Omar] al-Bashir, 'Fine for me to be subjected to an arrest warrant but what about Gaza?' And this is a plea one hears in the developing world repeatedly.

You ask us to take action against Sudan, Zimbabwe, Burma for human rights violations. And I believe that action should be taken against these states. But the developing world says, 'Why do you ask us to take action against these states when you yourself are engaged in the protection of Israel?' It's very difficult to know what's going to happen in this situation. I'm fairly disappointed about the United Nations. The General Assembly and the Human Rights Council have very little powers. The Secretary General of the United Nations is timid, shall we say. The Security Council is hampered by the veto, and the Quartet, whose very origin is suspect, is clearly under the control of the United States. In 2004, the International Court of Justice gave an advisory opinion holding the Wall as illegal. That has simply been ignored by the Security Council, the Secretary General, and the Quartet.

There are demands for another advisory opinion on the question of the consequences of prolonged occupation coupled with apartheid and colonialism. But again, such an opinion, even if given, is likely to be ignored. But I think there are some hopeful signs in respect of movements in civil society. We do see the question of action against Israel over Palestine being raised on university campuses, in churches and in trade unions. I do tend to get the impression that public opinion is beginning to shift, even though government policies remain much the same.

The Russell Tribunal on Palestine
1. Until when?

Nurit Peled

Nurit Peled-Elhanan teaches at the University of Tel Aviv. She is co- founder of Israeli-Palestinian Bereaved Parents for Peace. Her daughter, Smadar Elhanan, was killed in a suicide bombing attack in Jerusalem in 1997. In 2001, Dr Peled was awarded the Sakharov Prize for Human Rights and Freedom of Speech by the European Parliament.

These words are dedicated to the heroes of Gaza, the mothers and fathers and children, the teachers and doctors and nurses who are proving every day and every hour that no fortified wall can imprison the free spirit of men, women and children, and no form of violence can subdue life.

I was asked to speak here as an Israeli. As an Israeli I live in the same country the Palestinians live in, only on the other side of the wall. It is a very small country where Death has absolute dominion; where Death has had dominion for too long. And yet, the world, the whole wide world, is impotent against it. In the Jewish democratic state of Israel all human values have long been wiped away by the blood of innocent babes. Racist discourse is legitimate, and racist education is the only education allowed. Israeli children are raised on slogans such as love thy neighbour, while being trained to kill their neighbours, and their neighbours' children, demolish their houses, torture their elders, and deprive their ill and their dying of medical help and care. Jewish mothers raise their children with all the love and attention Jewish mothers have, and then rejoice when their children turn into murderers, and are proud when their children turn into corpses in uniform. In the Jewish democracy of Israel, 324 children, most of them kidnapped from their beds in the middle of the night by fully armed soldiers, are held in the inhuman conditions of Israeli prisons. In the Jewish democracy of Israel no one is ever punished for killing Palestinian children; Israeli governments trade in human life and in human blood, in a market where non-Jewish blood and bones are worth much less than Jewish ones; Israeli candidates who wish to be elected to the office of Prime Minister have to outscore their rivals in the killing of Palestinians, and make grand promises to kill and expel more and more and more. In the Jewish democracy of Israel 20% of the citizens of the state are labelled in schoolbooks a demographic problem, threat and even a demographic nightmare; their language, their culture, their rights and their hopes are erased from the face of the earth, both physically and symbolically.

Israel's attitude towards its Palestinian non-citizens has found its most horrifying expression in the ongoing pogrom that is still being carried out by the thugs of the Occupation army against the residents of the Gaza Strip. This is known to every one, and yet the world is powerless against it. The people of Gaza are still locked up in this immense prison, hungry, unemployed, ill and poor, with no means to escape or to better their lives in any way.

As an Israeli, it is very painful to me to realize the word Israel has become the synonym of Oppression, Tyranny, ruthless Apartheid and Racism, and that the Star of David is equated in rallies all over the world to the swastika.

I wish this tribunal will encourage people to arise and go to Gaza – the city of slaughter – or to any other city of oppression in Palestine to see with their own eyes the horrifying ghettoes in which these people are incarcerated, get married, have families, educate their children, and lead an impossible day to day life. I hope the free people of the world can have the courage to come to my country and defy all blockades and high walls and not give up until all barriers are broken and human dignity is restored.

But the siege of Gaza is only one of many sieges imposed today in the world by democratic powers as well as by non-democratic ones. All those sieges are meant for one purpose: to silence the voice of freedom and justice.

My co-laureate of the Sakharov Prize, Prof. Izzat Gazzawi, a man of peace in spite of the inhuman blows he suffered, who died of humiliation less than two years after receiving this prestigious award, wrote to me just before his heart surrendered, that he believed the Israeli soldiers who came to his house every night to break furniture and frighten the children wanted, in fact, to silence his voice. I have vowed then, as I believe we all should vow every day, to do everything within our power so that his and other such brave voices will not be silenced.

When the Jewish poet Bialik wrote after the Pogrom against the Jews in Kishiniev, '*Satan has not yet created Vengeance for the blood of a small child,*' it did not occur to him that the child might be a Palestinian child from the holy land, and his slaughterers – Jewish soldiers. And when he wrote:

> *Let the blood pierce*
> *through the abyss! Let the blood seep*
> *down into the depths of darkness, and*
> *eat away there, in the dark, and breach*
> *all the rotting foundations of the earth.*

he could not imagine that those foundations would be the foundations of the state of Israel, that a Jewish state would immerse all of us in the blood of little girls and boys up to our necks.

Today, when the most enlightened civilizations commit the most heinous crimes out of greed, megalomania and pure racism, Bialik's cry from a hundred years ago resonates once again:

> *And I, my heart is dead, no longer is there prayer*
> *on my lips;*
> *All strength is gone, and*
> *hope is no more.*
> *Until when,*
> *How much longer,*
> *Until when?*

2. Russell Tribunals

Ken Coates

The Russell Tribunal on Palestine was publicly launched at an international press conference in Brussels on 5 March 2009. Ken Coates, Chairman of the Bertrand Russell Peace Foundation, was asked to speak about previous Russell Tribunals. Video of the press conference is available online (www.russelltribunalonpal estine.com).

The Russell Tribunal on War Crimes in Vietnam was constituted on November 13th 1966 at a meeting in London. Russell was joined there by Jean-Paul Sartre, Vladimir Dedijer, Isaac Deutscher, and Lelio Basso, the distinguished Italian jurist, with a score of other notable men and women. At this meeting Russell said:

> 'The Tribunal has no clear historical precedent. The Nuremberg Tribunal, although concerned with designated war crimes, was possible because the victorious allied powers compelled the vanquished to present their leaders for trial. Inevitably the Nuremberg trials, supported as they were by State power, contained a strong element of *realpolitik* … our own task is more difficult … we do not represent any State power, nor can we compel the policy makers responsible for crimes against the people of Vietnam to stand accused before us. We lack *force majeure*. The procedures of a trial are impossible to implement.
> I believe that these apparent limitations are, in fact, virtues. We are free to conduct a solemn and historic investigation, uncompelled by reasons of State or other such obligations.'

It was difficult for the Tribunal to commence its work. Jean-Paul Sartre had wanted it to sit in Paris, and had asked President de Gaulle to agree to such a meeting. The request was denied. At first it seemed that the Tribunal would have nowhere to convene, but then the Swedish authorities gave their consent to an opening session in Stockholm. This was followed by another session in Copenhagen. The findings of the Tribunal were published right across the world, and made a notable contribution to the development of public opposition to the war. It became impossible to ignore the atrocities which marked that conflict, and it can be said that the Tribunal made an important contribution to allowing the plight of the Vietnamese people to be, in Russell's words, 'presented to the conscience of mankind'.

Subsequently, a second Tribunal was constituted to examine repressions in Latin America. This was initiated by Lelio Basso, and Edith Russell extended the initial invitations to those who agreed to serve in the investigations. After three sessions, a Permanent People's Tribunal was established, and this continued its work in response to popular requests from many countries. Russell had died in 1970, so that all this work had to be carried through without him.

But now there were many others who sought to emulate the Vietnam enquiries, some of them in concert with participants in the original tribunals, and some of them spontaneously. Those of us who had been involved in the first phases of the Russell Tribunal could not of course direct the spontaneous initiatives which grew up in different countries of the world. Some of them concerned matters of which we strongly approved, and some of them we found slightly strange, such as the enquiry announced in Yugoslavia into the regulation of international football tournaments.

But the intensification of conflict around the world, and particularly in the Middle East, gave rise to acute international disquiet. In February 2003, all this culminated in demonstrations in which millions of people opposed the planned invasion of Iraq. This overrode the opposition, unleashing 'shock and awe' against Iraqi cities and killing an estimated million people. Out of this came a World Tribunal on Iraq, with our explicit blessing, and a truly global range of participants. The final session of this Tribunal met in Istanbul at the end of June 2005. It, too, could not reach judgments that were binding in international law. But, in the words of Arundhati Roy:

> 'Our ambitions far surpassed that. The World Tribunal on Iraq places its faith in the consciences of millions of people across the world who do not wish to stand by while the people of Iraq are being slaughtered, subjugated and humiliated.'

A key participant in this enquiry was Professor Richard Falk, who has subsequently been appointed as the United Nations Special Rapporteur on the Situation of Human Rights in the Palestinian Territories Occupied since 1967. Professor Falk set out to visit Gaza and the West Bank in connection with his new duties, when, last December 14th, he was arrested and detained at Ben-Gurion airport by the Israeli authorities, following which he was summarily deported.

At the time, we were actively involved in the preparation of a new Tribunal on Palestine, being convened on the initiative of Pierre Galand and his colleagues. I wrote to Professor Falk about this, seeking his advice. Of course, he could not commit the UN to our support, but he did say:

> 'Given the manner in which the UN operates, I will have to keep my Special Rapporteur role separate from the great work you have presided over for so long at the Russell Peace Foundation. This whole direction of civil society vigilance with respect to state crimes that are exempted from accountability due to power politics has had a great influence on my work for many years.
>
> In the present situation, there is an unprecedented willingness of the UN System to acknowledge the importance of investigating whether war crimes have been committed in Gaza, and even the Secretary General has indicated that if the evidence supports the allegations, as it surely does, then accountability should follow. At the same time I anticipate that political forces will sustain the impunity of Israeli leaders, and that no mechanism of accountability will be established.
>
> In the light of this institutional vacuum, the role of civil society is crucial in establishing the grounds for the imposition of accountability in symbolic form. Such a proceeding, if well arranged, will also give additional support to the many initiatives now under way around the world involving boycotts, divestment, and the like, moves that were so effective in the anti-apartheid campaign. So I would encourage you to move ahead with your plans, perhaps placing emphasis on the plight of Gaza. Certainly any documentary record that emerges will be useful to me in preparing reports for the UN.'

3. The Situation in Palestine

Richard Falk

Richard Falk is the United Nations Special Rapporteur on the situation of human rights in the Palestinian territories occupied since 1967. He presented his report on the 'Human rights situation in Palestine and other occupied Arab Territories' to the Tenth Session of the United Nations Human Rights Council in Geneva in March 2009.

Summary

In the light of resolution S-9 adopted by the Human Rights Council at its ninth special session, the present report of the Special Rapporteur on the situation of human rights in the Palestinian territories occupied since 1967 focuses on the main international law and human rights issues raised by Israel military operations commencing on 27 December 2008 and ending on 18 January 2009. He challenges the widespread emphasis on whether Israeli force was disproportionate in relation to Palestinian threats to Israeli security, and focuses on the prior question of whether Israeli force was legally justified at all. He concludes that such recourse to force was not legally justified given the circumstances and diplomatic alternatives available, and was potentially a crime against peace.

The Special Rapporteur also gives relevance to the pre-existing blockade of Gaza, which was in massive violation of the Fourth Geneva Convention, suggesting the presence of war crimes and possibly crimes against humanity. He considers the tactics pursued during the attacks by both sides, condemning the firing of rockets at Israeli civilian targets, and suggests the unlawfulness of disallowing civilians in Gaza to have an option to leave the war zone to become refugees, as well as the charges of unlawful weapons and combat tactics. He recommends that an expert inquiry into these matters be conducted to confirm the status under international law of war crimes allegations, and to consider alternative approaches to accountability.

Finally, the Special Rapporteur insists that Israeli security and the realization of the Palestinian right of self-determination are fundamentally connected, and that the recognition of this aspect of the situation suggests the importance of an intensified diplomatic effort, respect by all parties of relevant international law rights, and implementation of the long deferred Israeli withdrawal from occupied Palestine as initially prescribed by the Security Council in its resolution 242 (1967). Until such steps are taken the Palestinian right of resistance within the limits of international humanitarian law and Israeli security policy will inevitably clash, giving rise to ever new cycles of violence. The Special Rapporteur also recommends action in response to the denial by Israel of entry to him on 14 December 2008.

* * *

I
Introduction

1. The present report does not have benefit from a recent mission to Gaza. Such a mission was planned and attempted in mid-December 2008, but was not carried out due to the denial of entry to the Special Rapporteur on the situation of human rights in the Palestinian territories occupied since 1967. The mission was to include a visit to the West Bank and East Jerusalem, and was supposed to commence with a scheduled meeting with the President of the Palestine Authority, Mahmoud Abbas. Entry was denied on 14 December 2008, the Special Rapporteur was detained in a facility close to Ben Gurion Airport, then expelled from Israel the day after. Such a refusal to cooperate with a United Nations representative, not to mention the somewhat humiliating treatment accorded (detention in a locked and dirty cell with five other detainees and excessive body search), has set an unfortunate precedent with respect to the treatment of a representative of the United Nations Human Rights Council, and more generally of the United Nations itself. This precedent should be seriously challenged for the sake of both the mandate and more broadly, to ensure that in future Member States accord appropriate respect and cooperation with official United Nations missions and activities. One possible form of challenge would be to seek an advisory opinion from the International Court of Justice as to the applicability of the Convention on the Privileges and Immunities of the United Nations. Since such an approach, even if undertaken, would not produce a result in the near future, it would also be important to seek a modification as soon as possible to the position of Israel via diplomatic channels.

2. The expulsion of the Special Rapporteur made information gathering on the ground impossible. In the light of resolution S-9/1 of the Human Rights Council adopted at the ninth special session, the report will focus on the main international law issues raised by Israel military operations commencing on 27 December 2008 and ending on 18 January 2009. It also considers implications for international criminal law, and discusses the underlying debate as to whether the attacks themselves were violations of the Charter of the United Nations, and international law. This broader inquiry is perhaps not strictly within the ambit of the mandate as a distinct subject matter, but its resolution bears directly on the interpretation of alleged violations of international humanitarian and human rights law, which in turn underpin contentions of war crimes and crimes against humanity, as well as implications for accountability and individual criminal responsibility.

II
Introductory clarification

3. A conceptual complexity arises from the nature of the participants in this conflict with respect to international law. International law governing the use of force has developed over time to regulate the behaviour of States in their relations with one another. Without in any way questioning the unity of the occupied Palestinian Territory, it is important to come to terms with the reality of Gaza as sealed off from the rest of occupied Palestine and not directly represented, given its present administrative structure, in international diplomatic arenas, such as the donors' conference at Sharm-al-Sheikh or in the United Nations. At the same time, the purposes of international law governing force is concerned with the protection of peoples and the preservation of peace, a sentiment echoed in Article 2 paragraph 4 of the Charter extended beyond relations among States by the phrase 'or in any other manner inconsistent with the purposes of the United Nations'. In the enumeration of purposes of the United Nations, Article 1 paragraph 1 affirms the obligation to resolve disputes by peaceful means 'in conformity with the principles of justice and international law'. These provisions, if read in the light of the Preamble to the Charter, clearly condition an assessment of any use of force in international relations that extends beyond the limits of territorial sovereignty. The decision of the International Court of Justice in the Nicaragua case extended this reasoning with regard to the inhibitions on defensive claims to use force to general international law beyond the framework of the Charter.

4. With regard to Gaza there is a further concern with respect to the

nature of the legal obligations of Israel towards the Gazan population. Israel officially contends that after the implementation of its disengagement plan in 2005 it is no longer an occupying power, and therefore is not responsible for observance of the obligations set forth in the Fourth Geneva Convention. That contention has been widely rejected by expert opinion, by the *de facto* realities of effective control, and by official pronouncements by for instance the United Nations High Commissioner for Human Rights and the Secretary-General (A/HRC/8/17), the General Assembly in its resolutions 63/96 and 63/98 and the Security Council in its resolution 1860. Since 2005, Israel has completely controlled all entry and exit routes by land and sea and asserted control over Gazan airspace and territorial waters. By imposing a blockade, in effect since the summer of 2007, it has profoundly affected the life and well-being of every single person living in Gaza. Therefore, regardless of the international status of the occupied Palestinian territory with respect to the use of force, the obligations of the Fourth Geneva Convention, as well as those of international human rights law and international criminal law, are fully applicable.

5. The final introductory clarification concerns the relations of international human rights law and international humanitarian law to international criminal law. Not every violation of human rights or infraction of the Geneva conventions constitutes a war crime or a crime of State. Moreover, criminal intent, by way of mental attitude or through circumstantial evidence, must be established. In essence, 'grave breaches' of the Geneva Conventions as defined in article 147 of the Fourth Geneva Convention normally provide a legal foundation for allegations of war crimes. It is to be noted that the role of international criminal law is to identify and implement the fundamental obligations of international humanitarian law in wartime, but also to take account of severe violations of human rights arising from oppressive patterns of peacetime governance.

6. The recommended scope of investigation should combine attention to violations of international humanitarian law, the laws of war, and general international law (treaty and customary) as it bears on the rights and duties of Israel as the occupying Power, and Hamas as the party exercising effective political control in Gaza at the present time. It is to be expected that Israel would cooperate with any investigation authorized by the United Nations in accordance with its obligations as a Member State under Article 56 of the Charter of the United Nations calling upon members to cooperate with the Organization, as well as the additional duties contained in the Convention on the Privileges and Immunities of the United Nations.

It is disquieting, however, to read that Prime Minister Ehud Olmert and other Israeli high officials have made formal statements to the effect of taking all necessary steps to protect any member of the Israel Defense Forces from being accused, and, if excused, to prevent indictment and prosecution.[1] Such sentiments seem inconsistent with any expectation of serious official cooperation with a proposed investigation. It may be necessary, given this prospect, to place greater reliance on respected nongovernmental organizations compiling evidence and submitting reports, and on formal interviews with qualified observers and witnesses.

III
Inherent illegality: Legally mandatory distinction between civilian and military targets impossible in large-scale sustained attacks on Gaza as commenced by Israel on 27 December 2008

7. It is the view of the Special Rapporteur that the most important legal issue raised by an investigation of the recent military operations concerns the basic Israeli claim to use modern weaponry on a large scale against an occupied population living under the confined conditions that existed in Gaza. This involves trying to establish whether, under the conditions that existed in Gaza, it is possible with sufficient consistency to distinguish between military targets and the surrounding civilian population. If it is not possible to do so, then launching the attacks is inherently unlawful, and would seem to constitute a war crime of the greatest magnitude under international law. On the basis of the preliminary evidence available, there is reason to reach this conclusion.

8. Considering that the attacks were directed at densely populated areas, it was to some extent inevitable and certainly foreseeable that hospitals, religious and educational sites and United Nations facilities would be hit by Israeli military ordinance, and that extensive civilian casualties would result. As all borders were sealed, civilians could not escape from the orbit of harm. For authoritative and more specific conclusions on these points, it will be necessary to mount an investigation based on knowledge of Israeli weaponry, tactics and doctrine to assess the degree to which, in concrete cases, it would have been possible, given the battlefield conditions, to avoid non-military targets and to spare Palestinian civilians to a greater extent. Even without this investigation, on the basis of available reports and statistics, it is possible to draw the important preliminary conclusion that, given the number of Palestinian civilian casualties and degree of devastation of non-military targets in Gaza, the

Israelis either refrained from drawing the distinction required by customary and treaty international law or were unable to do so under the prevailing combat conditions, making the attacks impossible to reconcile with international law. On the basis of existing information, the principal results of the military operation were as follows:

(a) A total of 1,434 Palestinian were killed. Of these, 235 were combatants. 960 civilians reportedly lost their lives, including 288 children and 121 women. 239 police officers were also killed; the majority (235) in air strikes carried out the first day. 5,303 Palestinians were injured, including 1,606 children and 828 women (namely 1 in every 225 Gazans was killed or injured, not counting mental injury, which must be assumed to be extensive);[2]

(b) Homes and public infrastructure throughout Gaza, especially in Gaza City, sustained extensive damage, including several United Nations facilities; an estimated 21,000 homes were either totally destroyed or badly damaged;

(c) A total of 51,000 people were internally displaced in makeshift shelters that provided minimal protection, while others fled to homes of friends and relatives that seemed slightly safer.[3]

9. There is no way to reconcile the general purposes and specific prescriptions of international humanitarian law with the scale and nature of the Israeli military attacks commenced on 27 December 2008. The Israeli attacks with F-16 fighter bombers, Apache helicopters, long-range artillery from the ground and sea were directed at an essentially defenceless society of 1.5 million persons. As recent reports submitted to the Council by the Special Rapporteur emphasized, the residents of Gaza were particularly vulnerable to physical and mental damage from such attacks as the society as a whole had been brought to the brink of collapse by 18 months of blockade that restricted the flow of food, fuel, and medical supplies to sub-subsistence levels and was responsible, according to health specialists, for a serious overall decline in the health of the population and of the health system. Any assessment under international law of the attacks of 27 December should take into account the weakened condition of the Gazan civilian population resulting from the sustained unlawfulness of the pre-existing Israeli blockade that violated articles 33 (prohibition on collective punishment) and 55 (duty to provide food and health care to the occupied population) of the Fourth Geneva Convention. Considering the obligation of the occupying Power to care for the well-being of the civilian occupied population, mounting a comprehensive attack on a society already weakened by unlawful occupation practices

would appear to aggravate the breach of responsibility described in the above owing to the difficulties of maintaining the principle of distinction.

10. The deputy head of the embassy of Israel at the European Union, Ambassador Zvi Tal, during discussions with a committee of the European Parliament, sought to defend the attacks on Gaza by describing them as addressing 'a very peculiar situation.' In responding to allegations about the bombing of United Nations schools in Gaza, he was quoted as saying: 'Sometimes in the heat of fire and the exchange of fire, we do make mistakes. We're not infallible.' This is deeply misleading in its characterization of the war zone. It is not a matter of mistakes and fallibility, but rather a massive assault on a densely populated urbanized setting where the defining reality could not but subject the entire civilian population to an inhumane form of warfare that kills, maims and inflicts mental harm that is likely to have long-term effects, especially on children who make up more than 50 per cent of the Gazan population.

IV
Non-exhaustion of diplomatic remedies, disproportionality, non-defensive nature of the attacks

11. It is a requirement of international customary law, as well as of the Charter of the United Nations, Article 2 paragraph 4 interpreted in the light of Article 1 paragraph 1 that recourse to force to resolve an international dispute should be a last resort after the exhaustion of diplomatic remedies and peaceful alternatives, even in circumstances where a valid claim of self-defence exists, absent a condition of urgency, assuming for the moment that an occupying power can ever claim a right of self-defense (for doubt about the availability of such a claim see para 28).[4] In the context of protecting Israeli society from rockets fired from Gaza, the evidence overwhelmingly supports the conclusion that the ceasefire in place as of 19 June 2008 had been an effective instrument for achieving this goal, as measured by the incidence of rockets fired and with regard to Israeli casualties sustained.

12. The graph on page 57, based on Israeli sources, shows the number of Palestinian rockets and mortar shells fired each month in 2008, with the period of the ceasefire stretching basically from its initiation on 19 June to its effective termination on 4 November when Israel struck a lethal blow in Gaza that reportedly killed at least six Hamas operatives. It dramatically demonstrates the extent to which the ceasefire was by far the most secure period with respect to the threats posed by the rockets.

13. The authors of a study based on the data displayed in the graph The above[5] concluded that 'the ceasefire was remarkably effective; after it

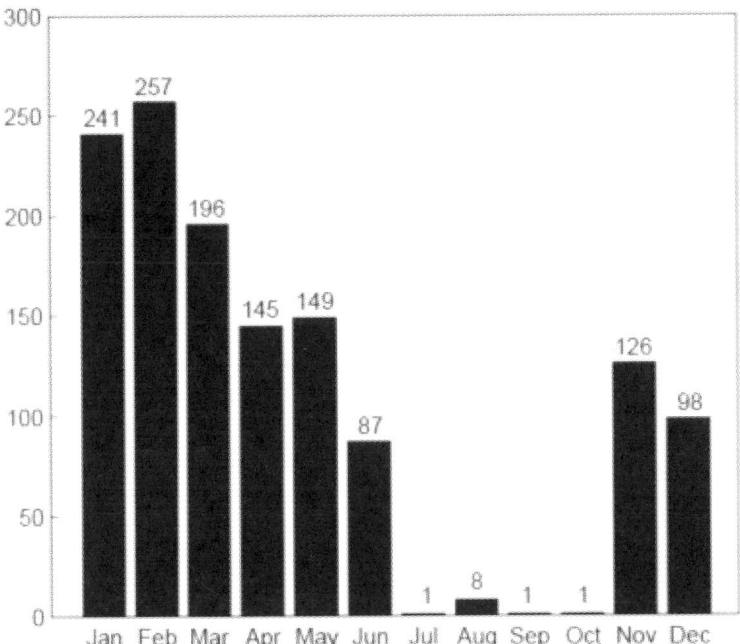

Number of Palestinian rockets and mortar shells fired in 2008

began in June 2008, the rate of rocket and mortar fire from Gaza dropped to almost zero, and stayed there for almost four months.' The experience of the temporary ceasefire demonstrates both the willingness and the capacity of those exerting control in Gaza to eliminate rocket and mortar attacks.

14. Beyond this, records show that, during the ceasefire, it was predominantly Israel that resorted to conduct inconsistent with the undertaking, and Hamas that retaliated. According to the above-mentioned study, during a longer period, from 2000 to 2008, it was found that, in 79 per cent of the violent interaction incidents it was Israel that broke the pause in violence. In the course of events preceding the attacks of 27 December, the breakdown of the truce followed a series of incidents on 4 November in which Israel killed a Palestinian in Gaza, mortars were fired from Gaza in retaliation, and then an Israeli air strike was launched that killed an additional six Palestinians in Gaza; in other words, the breakdown of the ceasefire seems to have been mainly a result of Israeli violations, although this offers no legal, moral or political excuse for firing of rockets aimed at civilian targets, which itself amounts to a clear violation of international humanitarian law.

15. Furthermore, Hamas leaders have repeatedly and formally proposed

extending the ceasefire, including for long periods. Khalid Mish'al writing in *The Guardian* on January 6, 2009 said 'When this broken truce neared its end, we expressed our readiness for a new comprehensive truce in return for lifting the blockade and opening all Gaza crossings, including Rafah.' It is notable that the President of the USA, Barack Obama, has called for this result in a statement accompanying his appointment of George Mitchell as Special Envoy on the Israel/Palestine conflict: 'As part of a lasting ceasefire, Gaza's border crossings should be open to allow the flow of aid and commerce.' This assertion is consistent with the call made by the Security Council in its resolution 1860 (2009) for 'unimpeded provision and distribution throughout Gaza of humanitarian assistance, including food, fuel, and medical treatment,' which in effect prescribes the end of the blockade of Gaza that has been maintained by Israel in violation of articles 33 and 55 of the Fourth Geneva Convention.

16. The continuing refusal of Israel to acknowledge Hamas as a political actor, based on the label of 'terrorist organization', has obstructed all attempts to implement human rights and address security concerns by way of diplomacy rather than through reliance on force. This refusal is important for reasons already mentioned (see para. 8 above), namely, that the population density in Gaza means that reliance on large-scale military operations to ensure Israeli security cannot be reconciled with the legal obligations under the Fourth Geneva Convention to protect to the extent possible the safety and well-being of the occupied Gazan population.

17. There are several relevant conclusions that demonstrate this link between relying on non-violent options and the requirements of international humanitarian law:

(a) The temporary ceasefire was impressively successful in shutting down cross-border violence and casualties on both sides;

(b) The Palestinian side adhered to the ceasefire, with relatively few exceptions, and relied on violence almost exclusively in reactive modes, while Israel failed to implement its undertaking to lift the blockade and seems mainly responsible for breaking lulls in the violence by engaging in targeted assassinations and other violent and unlawful provocations, most significantly by its air strike on 4 November 2008;

(c) The Hamas leadership appears ready at present to restore the ceasefire provided that the blockade is unconditionally lifted, which should in any event happen owing to its unlawful character, and should also be accompanied by guarantees against weapons smuggling on the Palestinian side, and a commitment to desist from targeted assassinations on the Israeli side;

(d) If substantiated by further investigation, this overall pattern prevailing at the time the attacks were launched would undermine the claim by Israel that its recourse to force was 'necessary' and 'defensive', both features of which must be present to support a valid claim under international law of self-defence;

(e) On the above basis, the contention that the use of force by Israel was 'disproportionate' should not divert our attention from the prior question of the unlawfulness of recourse to force. If for the sake of argument, however, the claim of self-defence and defensive force is accepted, it would appear that the air, ground, and sea attacks by Israel were grossly and intentionally disproportionate when measured against either the threat posed or harm done, as well as with respect to the disconnect between the high level of violence relied upon and the specific security goals being pursued. This legal sentiment is authoritatively expressed in Article 51(5)(b) of the Protocol I of the Geneva Conventions, in which prohibited disproportionate attacks are defined as 'an attack which may be expected to cause incidental loss of civilian life, injury to civilians, damage to civilian objects, or a combination thereof, which would be excessive in relation to the concrete and direct military advantage anticipated.' Israel did little to disguise its deliberate policy of disproportionate use of force, thereby acknowledging a refusal to comply with this fundamental requirement of international customary law. The Prime Minister of Israel was quoted after the ceasefire by the press agency Reuters as saying: 'The Government's position was from the outset that if there is shooting at the residents of the south, there will be a harsh Israeli response that will be disproportionate.'[6] To the extent that the Prime Minister's comment reflects Israeli policy, it was a novel and blatant repudiation of one of the most fundamental aspects of international law governing the use of force.

V
Refugee denial

18. In an unprecedented belligerent policy, Israel refused to allow the entire civilian population of Gaza, with the exception of 200 foreign wives, to leave the war zone during the 22 days of attack that commenced on 27 December. As the United Nations High Commissioner for Refugees stated on 6 January 2009, Gaza is 'the only conflict in the world in which people are not even allowed to flee.' All crossings from Israel were kept closed during the attacks, except for rare and minor exceptions. By so doing, children, women, sick and disabled persons were unable to avail themselves of the refugee option to flee from the locus of immediate harm resulting

from the military operations of Israel. This condition was aggravated by the absence of places to hide from the ravages of war in Gaza, given its small size, dense population and absence of natural or man-made shelters.

19. International humanitarian law has not specifically and explicitly at this time anticipated such an abuse of civilians, but the policy as implemented would suggest the importance of an impartial investigation to determine whether such practices of 'refugee denial' constitute a crime against humanity as understood in international criminal law. The initial definition of crimes against humanity, developed in relation to the war crimes trials after the Second World War, is 'murder, extermination, enslavement, deportation and other inhumane acts done against any civilian population'. More authoritative is the definition contained in Article 7(1)(k) of the Rome Statute, according to which crimes against humanity includes 'inhumane acts (…) intentionally causing great suffering, or serious injury to body or to mental or physical health.' Refugee denial under these circumstances of confined occupation is an instance of 'inhumane acts', during which the entire civilian population of Gaza was subjected to the extreme physical and psychological hazards of modern warfare within a very small overall territory. It should be kept in mind that this restriction on free movement, to escape from the war zone, was imposed on a population already severely weakened by the effects of the blockade.

20. The small size of Gaza and its geographic character also operated to deny most of the population remaining within its borders of an opportunity to internally remove itself from the combat zones. In this sense, the entire Gaza Strip became a war zone, although the actual combat area on the ground was more limited. In effect, leaving Gaza was the only way to remove oneself to a position of safety. In this respect, the option to become an internally displaced person was, as a practical matter, unavailable to the civilian population, although some civilians sought relative safety in shelters that were made available on an emergency basis for a tiny fraction of the population, mainly through the efforts of the United Nations Relief and Works Agency for Palestine Refugees in the Near East (UNRWA) and other United Nations and Non-Governmental Organizations' efforts. In some situations the shelters were not always treated as sanctuaries by the Israeli armed forces. Six UNRWA emergency shelters were damaged during Operation Cast Lead.[7]

21. Furthermore, given such emergency conditions, it seemed feasible to establish temporary refugee camps either in southern Israel or in neighboring countries for the duration of the attacks. This course of action had allowed almost one million Kosovars (almost half the civilian

population) to obtain temporary refuge in the neighbouring former Yugoslav Republic of Macedonia during the bombing by the North Atlantic Treaty Organization in 1999. It seems evident that, had Serbia denied the Kosovo population such a refugee option by controlling egress, it would have been accused of inhumane behaviour and criminality by the world community. It would seem that the law of war and international human rights law, for the sake of the protection of civilian innocence in wartime situations, needs to affirm the right of every non-combatant civilian to become a refugee, or at least to have the right to seek such a status, especially if the conditions for an internal 'refugee' option are not present.

22. Such an affirmation does not address the related question as to whether neighbouring countries have a legal duty to accommodate, to the extent feasible and at least temporarily, civilians seeking to escape from an ongoing war zone. It would seem at the very least that Israel as occupying Power and belligerent party had such a legal obligation. In a general way, such an obligation is set forth in articles 13 to 26 of the Fourth Geneva Convention. Especially relevant are article 15 which looks to the establishment of 'neutralized zones' to shelter the civilian population from 'the effects of war', article 16 which imposes a special duty to accord the sick and wounded, as well as expectant mothers, 'particular attention and respect', and article 24 which imposes a duty on the occupying Power to protect any children under 15 who are orphans or separated from their families, and obliges it to 'facilitate the reception of such children in a neutral country for the duration of the conflict'.

23. It is acknowledged that the particular circumstances in Gaza made it difficult, but not entirely impossible, to fulfill these obligations in the manner set forth in the Fourth Geneva Convention. What seems clear, however, is that Israel as occupying Power should have adapted these protective goals to the situation facing the population of Gaza, and that this was feasible to a considerable degree, at least to the minimum extent of allowing particularly vulnerable categories of persons within the civilian population, such as children, the sick and disabled, orphans, the elderly and the wounded, to leave. On 21 January 2009, the Executive Board of the World Health Organization reported, for instance, that more than half of the civilian casualties (over 1,300 dead and thousands injured) caused by the Israeli military operations were women, children, infants and elderly persons. This difficulty also gives weight to the argument (see paras 8-10 above) that contends that such a military operation, by its intrinsic nature, generates war crimes.

24. There are further implications with regard to upholding human

rights and international humanitarian law under wartime conditions. Confining the civilian population to the war zone also makes it more difficult, if not impossible, to sustain consistently the distinction between military and civilian targets, in combat situations. It also complicates an assessment of claims made by Israel that Hamas used civilians as human shields, and used civilian sites such as schools and mosques from which to engage in resistance. If civilians could not leave the war zone under such crowded conditions, some degree of intermingling would necessarily occur, especially in life and death situations.

VI
Expert inquiry on war crimes

25. There have been widespread calls for an investigation of the allegations of war crimes associated with the recent encounter in Gaza. The United Nations Secretary-General has called for such an investigation, urging that in the event that evidence of war crimes is found, mechanisms for accountability should be established. The High Commissioner for Human Rights has also supported an investigation of possible war crimes, recommending that it consider allegations of war crimes on both Israeli and Palestinian sides of the conflict. The Special Rapporteur does not propose another investigation but an expert inquiry to report on the implications of available evidence for international humanitarian law, especially the implications of war crimes of apparent violations. Such a report should also take into account the specific undertakings of the Human Rights Council. In contemplating such an inquiry, it is important that several factors be considered, including the preliminary question as to the applicable body of international law, and the concluding question regarding the availability of mechanisms of accountability. The inquiry should be conducted by three or more respected experts in international human rights law and international criminal law.

A. Scope of the inquiry

26. An inquiry, complementary to the fact-finding mission authorized by the Council in its resolution S-9/1, should be authorized to perform two basic tasks: to review all reports, including those pursuant to resolution S-9/1 results; and to establish, as definitively as possible, the facts underlying the main allegations of war crimes, including evidence in the form of eye-witness testimony, of contested battlefield practices, as well as explanations in exoneration or mitigation to the extent available, especially if provided by Israeli and Palestinian military commanders and political leaders. In other words, despite the apparent one-sidedness of the Gaza attack,

allegations of war crimes on both sides of the conflict should be taken into account. With respect to Hamas, this refers primarily to the factual profile relating to the rockets fired from its territory, including the determination of intent and issues of attribution (whether rockets were being fired by independent militias or even by groups opposed to Hamas). It would also need to consider all available evidence bearing on the types of weapons used and the combat circumstances of use. It would also be helpful if the inquiry report addressed such issues as the source of applicable rules of international criminal law by which to assess the evidence and that it recommend alternative procedures for establishing potential accountability on the part of individuals and political actors, especially with respect to the responsibility and capacity of the United Nations system. In this regard, legal uncertainties and political obstacles to the establishment of effective mechanisms should be acknowledged in the report.

27. It should be remembered that establishing evidence of the violation of international humanitarian law creates a non-criminal responsibility on the part of a State, and possibly of a non-State actor depending on the view taken with regard to the recent development of international treaty and customary laws of war, including the overall impact of Protocol I to the Geneva Conventions (1977) on the clarification of relevant legal norms. It should be made clear in the inquiry report that violations of the laws of war, even if grave breaches, do not automatically constitute war crimes or crimes against humanity or crimes against peace, although the Rome Statute in Article 8 treats all established grave breaches as war crimes. Potential legal accountability of political actors (including States) and individuals requires further assessment of whether the allegations and evidence appear to indicate violations of international humanitarian law and international human rights law and thus provide a solid basis in fact and law for charging the commission of international crimes.[8]

28. It is important that an inquiry in the context of the military operations initiated on 27 December 2008 and continuing until 18 January 2009, evaluate the allegations on both sides, including the issues of alleged criminality associated with both the decisions of the Government of Israel to launch the attacks and initiate a ground invasion of Gaza, as well as the circumstances surrounding the firing of rockets by Palestinian militants. It is further recommended that the underlying claim of Israel that it was acting in self-defence be evaluated in relation to the contention that such an attack violated Article 2 paragraph 4 of the Charter of the United Nations and amounted to an act of aggression under the circumstances, and whether the reliance on disproportionate use of force or the inherently indiscriminate

nature of the military campaign should be treated as a criminal violation of international customary and treaty law. There exists here a complex and unresolved issue as to whether an occupying power can claim 'self-defence' in relation to an occupied society, and whether its use of force, even if excessive, and of a border-crossing variety, can be regarded as 'aggression'. Israel seems to be barred from relying on its status as occupier considering that it claims that the occupation has ended, but of course the inquiry report need not respect that interpretation of the legal relationship.

29. There are difficult issues bearing on the status of what were called crimes against peace at the Nuremberg trials. On the one hand, the Rome Statute establishing the International Criminal Court does not yet include aggression or crimes against peace as falling within the competence of the tribunal due to the inability to agree upon a definition of aggression. In the event that there is agreement within the framework of the International Criminal Court, then the crime of aggression could be prosecuted (Article 5.2 of the Statute). On the other side of this question of the clarity of the anti-aggression norm embedded in crimes against peace is the majority decision of the British House of Lords in the recent case of Regina v. Jones and others, to the effect that the criminality of aggressive war established at Nuremberg remains firmly established in international customary law and its bearing on contested uses of force remains authoritative. This is an important issue that casts a shadow over the entire controversy about the Israeli attacks, and should be clarified to the extent possible in the inquiry report.

30. Other legal concerns relating to the inquiry and any accountability sequel involve the distinctive nature of the belligerent parties, including questions about the proper assessment of the legal responsibility of an occupying Power towards the occupied people from the perspective of international criminal law, the legal effects on the nature of Israeli criminal responsibility given its disengagement from Gaza in 2005, and the criminal responsibility under international law of a non-State actor that was exercising *de facto* administrative and governmental control during the period being investigated.

B. Applicable international criminal law

31. The applicable body of international criminal law for any investigation would include the jurisprudence compiled by the *ad hoc* International Criminal Tribunal for the Former Yugoslavia and the International Criminal Tribunal for Rwanda, which has fully examined violations of the laws of war, as contained in the jurisdictional statutes setting up such tribunals, established under the authority of the Security Council. It should

also include the list of international crimes enumerated in the Rome Statute of the International Criminal Court.

32. The crimes described in the London Agreement establishing the Nuremberg Tribunal in 1945 were subsequently confirmed as part of customary international law by the International Law Commission in 1950 under the rubric of 'Principles of International Law Recognized in the Charter of the Nuremberg Tribunal and in the Judgment of the Tribunal'.[9] These principles are treated by most international law experts as constituting 'peremptory norms' as defined in article 53 of the Vienna Convention on the Law of Treaties (1988): 'A peremptory norm of general international law is a norm accepted and recognized by the international community of States as a whole as a norm from which no derogation is permitted and which can be modified only by a subsequent norm of general international law having the same character.' Thus, if the Nuremberg categories of criminality qualify as peremptory norms embedded in international customary law, these crimes remain valid and relevant for the purpose of assessing the Israeli attacks under the labels of 'crimes against peace', 'war crimes', and 'crimes against humanity'. Reliance on the relevance of these crimes, especially crimes against peace, is singularly important to allow assessment of the underlying allegation that the Israeli attacks commencing on 27 December 2008 were intrinsically criminal because of their incapacity to maintain the distinction between military and civilian targets, a contention that Israeli political and military leaders challenge. If a solid basis in fact and evidence could be provided to back up this contention, it would provide the grounds for contending that the highest political and military leaders could potentially be held criminally responsible.

33. Alleged crimes associated with battlefield operations and command policy, such as the targeting of schools, mosques, ambulances, residential homes and health facilities, should be investigated to the extent possible, including evidence pertaining to the existence of deliberate intent or gross negligence. Extenuating circumstances should be taken into account, including allegations that buildings and their near surroundings were being used for combat purposes. It is important that this evidence be gathered quickly, and that the cooperation of the parties be solicited to the extent that the investigation establishes a prima facie case with respect to war crimes, and the responsible perpetrators can be identified, then the investigating report should either recommend that the parties be encouraged to establish criminal law procedures by which such individuals can be indicted, prosecuted, accorded due process and punished if found guilty, or propose some alternative mechanism. It is quite likely that the

investigation will be able to establish that certain practices and incidents have the characteristics of war crimes, but that it will be impossible to identify the supposed perpetrator(s), at least not without the cooperation of the parties engaged in combat.

34. Alleged crimes associated with legally dubious use of weaponry such as white phosphorous (which burns through clothing, sticks to skin and burns flesh to the bone), flachette bombs (which expel razor sharp darts), and Dense Inert Metal Explosives (DIME) bombs (causing intense explosions in a small area and body parts to be blown apart) should also be investigated. None of these weapons is, *per se*, explicitly banned by international law, but there is considerable support for the view that their use in dense urban areas where civilians are known to be or are habitually present would be a war crime. An investigation is needed to establish the extent of such use, and the specific circumstances under which use occurred. To the extent that a basis for criminal prosecution is established, the orbit of responsibility should focus on the command levels of decision with respect to policies and practices governing use, and generally accord serious, yet subordinate, attention to the identity of the low level perpetrators carrying out orders. Here too the cooperation of Israeli governmental authorities should be evaluated as a means of achieving accountability; if not regarded as reliable, alternative approaches should be recommended.

35. The practices of Hamas alleged to constitute war crimes should also be investigated, including the firing of rockets and mortar shells aimed at civilian targets; the alleged use of children and civilians as 'human shields'; and the abuse of the protected status of certain structures either to hide weaponry or as places of sanctuary for carrying on combat operations. The extent to which these latter practices are distinct crimes or serve to mitigate or excuse failures by Israel to respect the immunity of such targets needs to be determined. Here also, it is important to concentrate on the appropriate level of military and political command to determine the locus of possible criminality, and to recommend how accountability should be assessed.

C. Availability of mechanisms of accountability

36. An investigation should also address the mechanisms of accountability evaluated in terms of jurisdictional competence and political plausibility if it determines that substantial grounds for holding individuals and other political actors criminally responsible exist. Since Israel is not a State Party to the Rome Statute establishing the International Criminal Court, the most efficient mechanism for assessing accountability would be to establish, under the authority of the Security Council, an *ad hoc* criminal

tribunal for occupied Gaza, following the precedents of the 1990s (although this does not seem politically plausible under current conditions). It would also be theoretically possible for the Security Council acting under Chapter VII of the Charter to refer the situation to the Court for further action. It is arguable (although contested) that the General Assembly might establish such a tribunal by invoking its authority to 'establish such subsidiary organs as it deems necessary for the performance of its functions'. Whether such an initiative is related to the functions of the Assembly is an unresolved matter. There is also some question as to whether the fact that the Security Council, in its resolution 1860 (2009) 'decided to remain seized of the matter' makes it constitutionally inappropriate for the Assembly to take any action relating to the situation in Gaza resulting from the Israeli military operations.

37. Ideally, Israel, as the sovereign State exercising control over the territory where the alleged offences took place, should be the locus of judicial assessment, whether by its normal criminal law procedures or through the establishment of a special *ad hoc* process – but for reasons previously discussed (see para 6 above) this is extremely unlikely to take place. Nonetheless, human rights groups in Israel and occupied Palestine are compiling as much information as possible relating to allegations of war crimes to provide the legal grounds for recourse to national legal systems.

38. From the outlook of competence and plausibility, the most available accountability initiatives are associated with national criminal law procedures in those countries, such as Belgium and Spain, that give to their courts legal authority to prosecute war crimes under the rubric of universal jurisdiction, provided that the accused individual is physically present. It is likely that such an option would be influenced by the existence of a persuasive report under the auspices of the United Nations that recommended accountability.

39. The above mentioned situation has led the Minister for Justice of Israel, Daniel Friedman, to be designated to protect any Israeli detained abroad in accordance with the public pronouncement made by Prime Minister Olmert at a gathering of military officers a few days after the Gaza ceasefire went into effect: 'The Government will stand like a fortified wall to protect each and every one of you from allegations'. Israel also warned that it will take reprisals in the event that Israelis are arrested and charged abroad. Note that potential initiatives in national judicial settings are not limited to battlefield specific offences, but can be extended to encompass alleged crimes at the highest political and military levels of government. The case involving the indictment of former head of State of Chile, Augusto

Pinochet, adjudicated these issues in the Spanish and British legal systems, as well as in Chile itself, during the late 1990s and early 2000s.

VII
The broader settings of the attack

40. At the conclusion of the present report, it seems appropriate to reaffirm the connection between Israeli security concerns and the Palestinian right of self-determination. As long as Palestinian basic rights continue to be denied, the Palestinian right of resistance to occupation within the confines of international law and in accord with the Palestinian right of self-determination is bound to collide with the pursuit of security by Israel under conditions of prolonged occupation. In this respect, a durable end to violence on both sides requires an intensification of diplomacy with a sense of urgency, and far greater resolve by all parties to respect international law, particularly as it bears on the occupation as set forth in the Fourth Geneva Convention. Furthermore, it is important to acknowledge that the time has long passed for the implementation of Security Council resolution 242 (1967) requiring Israel to withdraw from Palestinian territories, for Israel to close unlawful settlements, desist from efforts to alter the demographics of East Jerusalem, respect the advisory opinion on the Wall of the International Court of Justice of 2004, and bring the occupation to a genuine end, either through negotiations or by unilateral action.

VIII
Recommendations

41. The Special Rapporteur recommends that:
(a) An advisory opinion on the obligations of a Member State to cooperate with special procedures of the Human Rights Council in relation to the application of Article 56 of the Charter of the United Nations and the relevant provisions of the Convention on the Privileges and Immunities of the United Nations be requested;
(b) A procedure for conducting an expert inquiry from the perspective of the role of the Human Rights Council into allegations of war crimes associated with Israeli military operations in Gaza from 27 December 2008 to 18 January 2009 be established;
(c) It be recognized that the Palestinian right of resistance under international law within the limits of international humanitarian law continually collides with Israeli security concerns as occupying Power, requiring basic adjustments in the relationship of the parties premised on respect for the legal rights of the Palestinian people; and that

sustainable peace in Gaza requires the permanent lifting of the blockade in the short term, and a diplomatic process that seeks peace in accordance with the requirements of international law in the long term.

References

1 'The soldiers and commanders who were sent on mission in Gaza must know that they are safe from various tribunals and that the state of Israel will assist them on this issue and defend them.', *Los Angeles Times*, 26 January 2009.
2 A recent report by Near East Consulting quoted by the Office for the Coordination of Humanitarian Affairs in its Gaza Humanitarian Situation Report of 26 January 2009 concluded that 96 per cent of Gaza residents suffer from depression, with intense depression being experienced by 81 per cent of the residents of North Gaza and Rafah districts. Such mental deterioration is itself an indication of a failure by the occupying power to discharge its basic duty to safeguard the health of civilians living under occupation.
3 Field Update from the Humanitarian Coordinator, 9 February 2009, and the Gaza Flash Appeal, 2 February 2009 of the Office for the Coordination of Humanitarian Affairs; as well as the Palestinian Centre for Human Rights, Press Release, Ref: 36/2009, 12 March 2009.
4 Of course, this analysis presupposes the rejection of the Israeli contention that Gaza has not been legally 'occupied' since the disengagement plan was implemented in 2005.
5 Nancy Kanwisher, Hohannes Haushofer, and Anat Biletzski, 'Reigniting Violence: How Do Ceasefires End?' 24 January 2009
6 See http://www.reuters.com/article/worldNews/idUSTE5100OY20090201
7 A much publicized instance was Beit Lahiya, where about 1,600 displaced Gazans had taken shelter at an UNRWA school, on which the UNRWA's spokesman said: 'Where you have a direct hit on an UNRWA school where about 1,600 people have taken refuge, where the Israeli Army knows the coordinates and knows who's there, where this comes as the latest in a catalogue of direct and indirect hits on UNRWA facilities, there have to be investigations to establish whether war crimes have been committed.', 'Israel declares ceasefire; Hamas say it will fight on', *New York Times*, 18 January 2009.
8 The International Court of Justice in the Bosnia Genocide Case made clear that a state can be held legally responsible for the commission of the crime of genocide, although only individuals can be prosecuted, convicted, and punished for violations of international criminal law (Application of the Convention on the Prevention and Punishment of the Crime of Genocide (Bosnia and Herzegovina v. Yugoslavia), paragraphs 142-201). Such a reference is intended solely to clarify the issue of potential state responsibility, and is not meant to imply directly or indirectly that the Israeli military operations in Gaza could be construed as 'genocide.'
9 Yearbook of the International Law Commission, 1950, vol. II, para. 97.

Viva Palestina

George Galloway MP

George Galloway, Member of Parliament for Bethnal Green and Bow, dissects the Charity Commission's obstruction of his remarkable efforts to provide help for Gaza. We reprint his open letter in full.

To the Charity Commission,

I have been travelling for many weeks in North Africa and the Middle East, Europe, and North America. I have returned to a London address I seldom visit to find a blizzard of correspondence from you. Your correspondence, when read together, as I have just done, seems to represent a wildly disproportionate and inappropriate reaction to our recent delivery of aid to the suffering Palestinians in Gaza, and must raise the question: Why?

The peremptory letters from you, and by you I mean the Charity Commission, are full of bluster and threat, issuing absurd deadlines to people it does not seem to occur to you are not even receiving your letters, either because they are working abroad (Ms Razuki and Mr Al-Mukhtar), travelling abroad on high profile political business (myself), or you are writing to them at the wrong address.

In my own case, Easter Saturday opened with your, latest, threat to go before a High Court judge in a bid to force me to appear before you. That will not be necessary. I look forward to telling you to your faces what I think of you. Which is this.

I have become increasingly concerned about the abuse of your powers displayed in your brazenly obvious political double standards. About your attempts, under the guise of regulating British charities, to police the democratic efforts of political activists in Britain in a way never envisaged by Parliament. About your preparedness to waste large sums of public money in political stunts, either at the behest of others or in the hope that you are properly anticipating their wishes. And above all, in the context of this issue, your almost laughably obvious prejudice against the Palestinian cause, and against Britain's two million-strong Muslim community.

Just one example will suffice for now, although I have more, much more.

During Israel's 22-day attack on virtually defenceless Palestinian civilians in Gaza – condemned by virtually everyone in the world from the United Nations to the Pope and including the British government – an organization, The Zionist Federation, took out a full page advert in the *Jewish Chronicle* on 9th January asking readers to send 'care packages' to 'our [i.e. Israeli] soldiers fighting on the front line' in Gaza, and to send charity vouchers to a British registered charity, Operation Wheelchairs Committee (charity number 263089), for the same purpose.

Although this was immediately drawn to your attention, you appear to have done absolutely nothing at all about such an abuse of charitable status. The Zionist Federation is presumably not a registered charity, any more than Viva Palestina was. The Zionist Federation appeal was for money for 'care packages' with donations possible online to www.zionist.org.uk, and to the charity Operation Wheelchairs Committee. By the logic of your actions towards Viva Palestina, surely you should have immediately declared the Zionist Federation to be a charity with all that that entails. But you did not do so. Why? In any case, the Operation Wheelchairs Committee is a charity, soliciting for funds in this advert to support a foreign army involved in a widely condemned military action, in which thousands of civilians were killed, maimed and orphaned. Yet the Charity Commission did nothing. No freezing of bank accounts, no press releases, no carefully briefed 'concerns', no threats of High Court judges.

It will only take the reader (I am publishing this letter as widely as I can) a moment's thought to imagine what the Charity Commission's attitude would have been if a British – Muslim – Charity had taken a full page advertisement in a different British newspaper, raising money for 'care packages' for 'our [i.e. Palestinian] soldiers fighting on the front line' in Gaza.

Not only would you have gone into overdrive and immediately begun freezing their assets; the hue and cry in the press you would have fed, would have seen the charity's trustees under arrest.

This is an incontestable example of your persistent bias. Because, in contrast to your inaction on a British charity raising money for the Israeli army, and in the absence of such a hypothetical Muslim charity, you have launched this hysterical campaign to try and wreck the work of Viva Palestina instead.

Without any knowledge of the intentions of Viva Palestina, and on the basis of press reports, you pronounced, as is your wont, that we were in effect a charity, to give yourselves locus in our affairs. You misunderstood – I believe deliberately – the structure of our Gaza convoy, purporting to believe that we – the subscribers (whatever that means) – were holding more than a million pounds about which you expressed 'concerns', when, in fact, as you have been told but continue to ignore, this was never the case.

You first frightened the banks into refusing our attempts to open a bank account. When we finally found a bank which would allow us to open an account, you intimidated them into freezing it, I believe exceeding your powers. You then began procuring documents – possibly illegally – about us from the Islamic Bank. As a result of your press briefings about your 'concerns', newspapers began to refuse to accept advertisements from us, donors turned away, and the public were encouraged to believe that Viva Palestina was something to be avoided – conjuring-up an undisclosed but lurking suspicion about it.

In all this you acted not as the public would expect a Charity Commission to do, but rather as a self-appointed state policeman of the activist sector, a mission-creep towards a style of work which simply must be contested.

Here are the facts. Accept them and save the public purse a lot of money it can't afford. And get off the backs of Britain's Muslims and the Palestinian people.

I am not a trustee of Viva Palestina. You say I am a 'subscriber', though you do not say what that means. I have nothing to do with Viva Palestina's finances, I am not a signatory to its frozen bank account. I will attend the meeting with you, because I intend to launch a parliamentary campaign, and take it to the country, to put you back in your place.

I did inspire the creation of Viva Palestina, and I am very proud of that. If those running it listen to me, they will refuse to take anything off their website at your behest. The example you cite of an item which should be taken down, could just as easily have been any one of a hundred items. And would become so, once your right to dictate the activities of a political campaigning organisation was conceded.

For that is what Viva Palestina was, and is. Its constitution – its actual constitution, not the one you wish it had – makes this abundantly clear. So does everything it says and does. If all that renders Viva Palestina not eligible to be a charity, then that's fine. Let me emphasise this as strongly as I am able. Viva Palestina does not want to be a charity.

It is you, for transparently political reasons, who insisted that charitable status should be sought. You registered Viva Palestina as a charity in record quick time, and without the great bulk of the information you normally require. And then you froze the record-quick new charity's bank account so that it could not operate. These are police state tactics, entirely inappropriate and without any basis.

Viva Palestina simply provided a focus for an aid convoy from Britain to Gaza. It was de-centralised. Each participant was responsible for raising their own money, bringing their own vehicles, filling their own vehicles with their own aid, making their own donations in Gaza. You have been told this, but continue to misrepresent the position. The money raised by Viva Palestina itself – a much smaller amount – was publicly declared to be intended as a donation to a British charity for work in Gaza – Interpal, with which you are depressingly familiar, having harassed it for years on repeatedly debunked smears.

The vast majority of the participants in the convoy, and the vast majority of those who helped them with money and aid, were British Muslims.

Having exerted that mighty effort, those British Muslims now find that their peaceful democratic response to the crisis in Gaza has been criminalised by you, and their aid confiscated. This all follows the high-profile police raid on vehicles from the Muslim community in the North West, heading to join the convoy the night before its departure. This raid, blazed across the media, saw the arrest of ten Muslims headed for the convoy. All ten of them were later released without charge, but not before sowing the seeds of tremendous bitterness in the communities from which the men came.

This is dangerous as well as foolish. There are extremists on the edge of the Muslim community even now saying 'I told you so' to those who had been naïve enough to think Britain was still the kind of country where efforts like ours could be appreciated and, at least, be free from the kind of arbitrary and unjust actions taken by you. These actions undermine the confidence of British Muslims in the democratic system in Britain, and are therefore dangerous and against the interests of our country.

I understand from my colleagues that you have now frozen more than £100,000 intended to help the suffering Palestinian people. Shame on you. I suppose it is too much to hope that you might have that on your conscience. But be sure I intend to let as many people as possible know, here and abroad, what you have done.

Viva Palestina's work has effectively come to a halt since your intervention in its affairs, and in my absence. This was, I'm sure, your intention. Viva Palestina has not spent any money improperly. It would not do so. Indeed, it could not do so. It has spent hardly anything at all – thanks to you. But it intends to get its money back from you. Viva Palestina have instructed lawyers to deal with you, and a barrister will accompany us to the meeting with you. If necessary, we will start a new organization, free from your wrecking efforts. But we want this money back, please be sure about that. There are Palestinians dying as a result of the malignant, sinister, cynical actions taken by you. Trust me, you'll be hearing more about this.

Yours faithfully,
George Galloway MP

Lions led by BBC donkeys

'The BBC Trust's report on Jeremy Bowen's dispatches from the Middle East is pusillanimous, cowardly, outrageous, factually wrong, and ethically dishonest. But I am mincing my words. The Trust – how I love that word which so dishonours everything about the BBC – has collapsed, in the most shameful way, against the usual Israeli lobbyists who have claimed – against all the facts – that Bowen was wrong to tell the truth ... And this, remember, is the same institution which said that to broadcast an appeal for medicines for wounded Palestinians in Gaza might upset its "neutrality" ... How do we solve this problem? Well I can certainly advise viewers to turn to Sky TV's infinitely tougher coverage of the Middle East and – I admit I contribute to this particular station – I can recommend the courage with which Al-Jazeera English covers Gaza and the rest of the Palestinian-Israeli war. I can well see how BBC executives will say this article of mine today is "over the top". Jeremy Bowen may indeed think the same. But the First World War metaphor would be correct. For Bowen and his colleagues are truly lions led by BBC management donkeys.'

Robert Fisk, The Independent, 16 April 2009

Licence to Torture

Tony Simpson

We first featured Barton Gellman's revelations about rendition and torture, made in the Washington Post in December 2002, in Spokesman 81, *entitled* Dark Times. *Gellman has pursued this subject with notable persistence. It forms a central theme of* Angler: The Shadow Presidency of Dick Cheney, *recently published by Allen Lane (price £25). 'Angler' is the US Secret Service's code name for Cheney. Tony Simpson is the assistant editor of* The Spokesman.

During the spring and summer of 2001, the Bush Administration ignored a series of high-level warnings about an imminent and large-scale attack in the United States. Then, on September 11th, the twin towers of the World Trade Center in New York collapsed after two aircraft were flown into them, killing 2,750 people, a third aircraft ploughed into the Pentagon in Washington DC, killing still more, whilst a fourth crashed in a field in Pennsylvania, killing all on board.

The Administration appeared in deep disarray. President Bush had been reading a story to schoolchildren in Florida when news of the attacks reached him, whilst Vice President Dick Cheney had to be frog-marched by secret service agents to a secure bunker in Washington. At that time, it was thought that a fourth plane was still heading towards the White House, intent unknown, whilst various other aircraft had yet to respond to air traffic control's urgent requests for information. The phones and video links in Cheney's bunker didn't work properly. The Vice President was waiting to speak to his President, who was quickly airborne himself. Each time the phone rang, Cheney lifted the receiver and said 'yello'. But the call was for someone else. A photograph in Barton Gellman's new book *Angler* shows Cheney taking one of those calls in the Bunker, while National Security Advisor Condoleezza Rice looks on, brow furrowed. Cheney's key advisor, lawyer David Addington, stands nearby.

But if the Bush Administration collectively was unprepared for 9/11, Vice President Cheney was in no doubt about what response to the attack was necessary.

The country was at war, the enemy was within the United States as well as outside, and exceptional methods were required. Within the space of a few weeks, the US was bombing Afghanistan, and hunting Osama bin Laden, the leader of the al Qaeda network thought to be behind the 9/11 attacks. US and British special forces were confronting the Taliban, which had ruled Afghanistan and given hospitality and protection to Osama and his cohorts.

What was to be done with prisoners taken during the fighting in Afghanistan? What was their status under international law? Little if any proper preparation had been made for such an eventuality. Very quickly, the US government was embarked on a reckless course that was to lead, ultimately, to systematic torture of so-called 'high-value targets' at Guantanamo Bay, and the extraordinary abuses, many of them sexual in character, of inmates held at Abu Ghraib prison in Iraq. How was it that their moral descent was so rapid and so deep?

According to Barton Gellman's account, on September 11th itself, Cheney asked his legal advisor, David Addington, to address the question 'what new authority will the president need?' Already, the Vice President knew the gloves were coming off, and exceptional measures were to be used, both internationally and at home in terms of surveillance of US citizens and their communications. Might there be another cell in the US preparing a chemical, biological, or even a nuclear 9/11?

Addington sprang into action, working with others, particularly in the Office of Legal Counsel, which arbitrates when US government agencies disagree about what the law means. Its opinions are binding on all cabinet departments. It was John C. Yoo of the Justice Department who wrote, two weeks after 9/11, that no law

> 'can place any limits on the President's determinations as to any terrorist threat, the amount of military force to be used in response, or the method, timing, and nature of the response. These decisions, under our Constitution, are for the President alone to make.'

Cheney and Addington found Yoo's analysis 'congenial', according to Gellman. The existence of this new legal framework, according to Cheney, was to be concealed as much as possible from legislative or judicial actors who might object.

What was all this to mean for the prisoners captured in Afghanistan? The Taliban surrendered the town of Mazar-i-Sharif to General Dostum's Northern Alliance on 9 November 2001. Extensive US airstrikes helped precipitate the surrender, which happened much quicker than anticipated. There were hundreds of prisoners. What was to be done with them?

On 13 November, Bush met privately with Cheney over lunch at the White House. Cheney had with him a proposal drafted by David Addington, his legal advisor. Its gist, according to Gellman (p.163), was to strip foreign suspects of access to any court – civilian or military, domestic or foreign. They could be confined indefinitely without charge. They would be tried, if at all, in closed 'military commissions', modelled on the ones Franklin Roosevelt set up for Nazi saboteurs in World War Two.

The next day, Cheney told the US Chamber of Commerce that a terrorist does not 'deserve to be treated as a prisoner of war'. It was ten weeks later, following a sharp dispute within the Administration, that Bush ratified the policy that Cheney had declared: the Geneva Conventions would not apply to al Qaeda or Taliban fighters captured on the battlefield. Donald Rumsfeld, Cheney's ally at the Department of Defense, publicly endorsed the new line, declaring all captured fighters in Afghanistan 'unlawful combatants' who 'do not have any rights' under Geneva.

The Vice President and his collaborators may have had in mind at this time what was happening at Mazar. Rumsfeld had intervened to prevent the negotiated release of foreign fighters: 'It would be most unfortunate if the foreigners in Afghanistan – the al Qaeda and the Chechens and others who have been there working with the Taliban – if those folks were set free and in any way allowed to go to another country and cause the same kind of terrorist acts', he said. As a result, around 470 people were taken to the Kalai Janghi fort near Mazar, where Dostum had his headquarters, and incarcerated in the tunnels below one of its giant compounds. Many of them were subsequently killed by British and American special forces, following an attempted breakout which coincided with the arrival of CIA interrogators on 25 November. (For the full story, see Jamie Doran's article 'Massacre at Mazar' in *Spokesman 77*.)

Meanwhile, lawyers at the National Security Council were alarmed at the implications of Cheney's new approach. John Bellinger warned Condoleezza Rice:

> '… even the closest allies could be expected to stop handing over suspects to US custody. Faxes had been pouring in from overseas since Bush signed the order for military commissions. The first one had come from the British lord chancellor, noting pointedly that London's co-operation was based on accepted legal norms.'

Of course, the British were already closely involved in the emerging 'war on terror'. Tony Blair, then Prime Minister, had abandoned his speech to the Trades Union Congress, scheduled for 11 September, in order to concentrate on that 'war'. The situation was developing quickly across the Atlantic in Washington. In a matter of weeks, the hunt was on for locations to hold and interrogate 'unlawful combatants' which were beyond the reach of those who police international law. The British Indian Ocean Territory of Diego Garcia, which already served as a massive US military installation, was considered and apparently rejected in favour of Guantanamo as a long-term solution because, according to Karen Greenberg, author of *The Least Worst Place*,

> 'Europe posed a particular problem. Not only would the relocation of prisoners there require negotiations and the consent of the host country to conditions and practices, but the European Court of Human Rights would inevitably become involved.'

(It was not until 2008 that the British Foreign Secretary, David Miliband, finally admitted that the US had indeed used Diego Garcia for the rendition of detainees.)

Cheney and his allies wanted to construct what has been described as the 'legal equivalent of outer space' – a place where detainees had no status, where no rules and no jurisdiction applied. The US installation at Guantanamo Bay on the island of Cuba was to be enrolled for this purpose.

Now, the debate focused on how to extract information quickly from detainees. Gellman records how Cheney had taken a close interest in the fate of William Buckley, CIA station chief in Beirut, who was captured in Lebanon in the 1980s. Buckley knew a lot about CIA operations in the Middle East and, under torture, revealed details to his captors. The lesson Cheney appeared to draw from Buckley's experience was that torture worked. Of course, this presupposes that the person being tortured has useful information to impart:

> 'No longer was the vice president focused on procedural rights, such as access to lawyers and courts. The subject now was elemental: How much suffering could US personnel inflict on an enemy to make him talk – "quickly"?' (Gellman, p175)

Parts of the US Administration became embroiled in detailed discussions about what cruelties were permissible, and which were not. A line was drawn at burying people alive, but water-boarding to simulate drowning was endorsed, as were other practices:

> 'It took four months for Yoo to produce a formal opinion. Meanwhile – in secret consultations with Gonzales, Flanigan, Addington, and CIA lawyers – Yoo gave interim authority for most of what the agency wanted to do. According to an authoritative source, Yoo rejected one proposed technique: the

CIA could not bury a subject alive, even if it planned to dig him back up in time. Convincing a person of his imminent death was torture, open and shut. Other proposed methods, Yoo said, were fine.' (p.177)

Gellman goes on to record the extraordinary behaviour of senior members of President Bush's Administration:

'Beginning in the second quarter of 2002 – and periodically until at least early 2005, … Cheney and Rice and the war cabinet sat with George Tenet and his successor in the Situation Room. The vice president led meetings with Don Rumsfeld, Colin Powell, and John Ashcroft, among others, to decide which torments exactly would be inflicted on each of the "high-value detainees".' (p.178)

One such detainee was Mohammed Qahtani who, it was thought, had tried to meet with Mohammed Atta, one of the main instigators of the 9/11 attacks. What did he know about possible future attacks on the US? A lengthy request for permission to begin 'more aggressive' forms of questioning was prepared. Eighteen techniques that interrogators might use were listed, ranging from water-boarding to hooding and yelling, isolation, stress positions, 24 hour interrogations, and the use of 'individual phobias (such as fear of dogs) to induce stress'.

Qahtani was abused by his interrogators for more than seven weeks, with three teams working shifts 20 hours a day. The torture methods, and his responses, were recorded in a log. According to Gellman:

'On the fiftieth day, Navy general counsel Alberto Mora threatened to file an official written protest, saying the methods employed against Qahtani "constituted, at a minimum, cruel and unusual treatment and, at worst, torture". Rumsfeld rescinded authority for the new methods the same day.' (p.188)

What were the British doing during this time? Binyam Mohamed, who has recently returned to Britain from Guantanamo Bay, has begun to shed some light on this question. He was first detained in Pakistan in April 2002, whilst trying to board a flight to Britain. During the next seven years, he was rendered first to Morocco, then to Afghanistan, and finally to Guantanamo Bay. British intelligence officers were actively engaged with his interrogation from the beginning, interviewing him face-to-face in Pakistan. Subsequently, they supplied information and questions to his Moroccan torturers. Indeed, Binyam Mohamed believes that it was the British who urged his rendition to Morocco because he lived amongst the Moroccan community in London. Mr Mohamed describes his worst time in the black prison in Afghanistan, where he was kept in complete darkness for weeks on end. Eventually, he was transported again from Afghanistan to Guantanamo, where he spent several years. Finally, with the help of his

British lawyer, Clive Stafford Smith of the organisation Reprieve, and an American military lawyer, he was allowed to leave Guantanamo and return to Britain. Now he can give first-hand testimony about Britain's role in the rendition and torture industry that burgeoned during the years following 9/11, when Cheney took charge as 'Shadow President'.

U.S. Department of Justice

Office of Legal Counsel

Office of the Assistant Attorney General   Washington, D.C. 20530

August 1, 2002

Memorandum for John Rizzo
Acting General Counsel of the Central Intelligence Agency

Interrogation of al Qaeda Operative

As part of this increased pressure phase, Zubaydah will have contact only with a new interrogation specialist, whom he has not met previously, and the Survival, Evasion, Resistance, Escape ("SERE") training psychologist who has been involved with the interrogations since they began. This phase will likely last no more than several days but could last up to thirty days. In this phase, you would like to employ ten techniqlies that you believe will dislocate his expectations regarding the treatment he believes he will receive and encourage him to disclose the crucial information mentioned above. These ten techniques are: (1) attention grasp, (2) walling, (3) facial hold, (4) facial slap (insult slap), (5) cramped confinement, (6) wall standing, (7) stress positions, (8) sleep deprivation, (9) insects placed in a confinement box, and (10) the waterboard. You have informed us that the use of these techniques would be on an as-needed basis and that not all of these techniques will necessarily be used. The interrogation team would use these techniques in some combination to convince Zubaydah that the only way he can influence his surrounding environment is through cooperation. You have, however, informed us that you expect these techniques to be used in some sort of escalating fashion, culmillating with the waterboard, though not necessarily ending with this technique. Moreover, you have also orally informed us that although some of these teclmiques may be used with more than once, that repetition will not be substantial because the techniques generally lose their effectiveness after several repetitions. You have also informed us that Zubaydah sustained a wound during his capture, which is being treated.

In April 2009, President Obama released four lengthy 'torture memos' sent from his predecessor's Office of Legal Counsel to legal officers of the CIA, in 2002 and 2005. This excerpt from a memo written by Jay S. Bybee, Assistant Attorney General, dated 1 August 2002, concerns the interrogation of Mr Abu Zubaydah, who was subsequently waterboarded 83 times during that month.

I Disown this Government

Bryan Gould

Bryan Gould was Member of Parliament for Southampton Test during the 1970s, and subsequently for Dagenham from 1983 to 1994,when he resigned and returned to New Zealand to become Vice-Chancellor of Waikato University. In 1992, John Smith had defeated him in the contest for the Labour Party leadership. This article was published in The Guardian in February 2009.

Those, like me (and almost everyone I know in the Labour Party), who have been critical over the years of New Labour and its record in government might have expected that the passage of time would bring with it a kinder judgment. And in my case, in particular, it might have been thought that – twelve thousand miles away – distance would lend enchantment.

How, then, to explain that the more we take the long view of the Blair and now the Brown government, the sharper seem the contours of its failures and betrayals? How is it that the features of its landscape that grow – as our perspective lengthens – in shocking, anger-making prominence are those shameful episodes at home and abroad which cumulatively are a complete denial of what a Labour government (or any British government) should have been about?

There have been, of course, many good and decent day-by-day achievements of this government. Across the whole range of political issues, I do not say that Britain did not do better under Labour than it would have done under most alternatives. But these achievements have been molehills, judged against the towering peaks scaled by New Labour in its rejection not only of Labour, but also of any decent and civilised values.

The first – and for that reason perhaps most unexpected – contravention of civilised norms was the Iraq war. The damning judgment of that doomed enterprise has been repeatedly rehearsed, but to read the charge sheet again is still a shocking experience. A British Prime Minister, claiming the right to moral leadership and an almost religious duty to confront evil, sucked up to a soon-to-be discredited US President, and helped to launch an invasion of a distant country – an invasion based upon a lie, and one that flew in the face of international law, undermined the United Nations, alienated the whole of the Muslim world, seemed to validate the claims of terrorists and those who recruited them, destroyed the country that was invaded and killed hundreds of thousands of its citizens, took many young soldiers to unnecessary deaths, and rightly reduced Britain's standing in the world.

The New Labour government still refuses to acknowledge that any of this was wrong. It will not even countenance an independent inquiry into how such a fatal mistake was made.

It may seem improbable that the scale of the Iraq calamity could be matched in any other area of government. Yet, as the reasons for and scale of the global recession become clear, it is also increasingly apparent that another global (as well as British) disaster can be laid – substantially, if only partly – at the door of the New Labour government.

It was, after all, that government which enthusiastically endorsed the virtues of the 'free' market, which turned its back on the need for regulation, which celebrated the excesses of the City, which proclaimed that it was 'intensely relaxed about people becoming filthy rich'. The government that should have protected the interests of ordinary people was dazzled by the super-rich; unsuspecting Labour supporters found themselves thrown on the tender mercies of a market-place that was cleared of any limits that might have restricted the rich and powerful. There have been no more enthusiastic cheer-leaders for the culture of greed and excess than New Labour ministers.

On the central issue of politics – the willingness of government to use its democratic legitimacy to intervene in the market in order to restrain its excesses – the New Labour government ensured that the dice lay where they fell, and applauded as they did. It was Tony Blair who, standing shoulder to shoulder with Rupert Murdoch, proclaimed that the future lay with the 'globalisers', and that those who wanted to reclaim some control over their lives were 'isolationists, nationalists and nativists'. It was Gordon Brown who removed the major economic decisions from democratic control, and handed them over to unaccountable bankers.

That betrayal of those who looked to a Labour government to help them has seen a rapid widening of inequality and a sharp intensification of social disintegration. It is the jobs, homes and lives of ordinary people that have borne the brunt. The country is a weaker and poorer place as a result.

But even that failure pales by comparison with the latest revelations about the abandonment by New Labour of any pretence to civilised standards. We now know that this government connived with the Bush administration to hold people illegally, to kidnap them in secret, and to torture them while in custody – all in the name of a war against the forces of darkness. The perpetrators of these outrages seem to believe that they can be washed clean by simply declaring their superior morality.

Nothing more clearly distinguishes those beyond the pale than their willingness to use the secret, illegal and cowardly infliction of pain to terrify, cow and bend to their will helpless people being held without charge or trial or legal redress. It beggars belief that any British government could, in a supposed democracy, do so, and not even bother to respond to its critics. It is simply incredible that a Labour government, claiming to represent the values of the Labour movement, could believe in these circumstances that it has any right to remain in office.

For me, this is too much. I am sick to the stomach. I disown this so-called Labour government. I protest.

www.bryangould.net

ASLEF the train drivers' union

www.aslef.org.uk

Let's use May Day to get the UK back on track ...

**Celebrate the skills of working people
Honour our achievements and
Secure our share of the country's wealth**

Keith Norman
General Secretary

Alan Donnelly
President

Reviews

Adam Smith in Beijing

Giovanni Arrighi, *Adam Smith in Beijing: Lineages of the Twenty-first Century*, 432 pages, Verso, paperback ISBN 9781844672981, £14.99

Giovanni Arrighi has added to his big book, *The Long Twentieth Century*, and his subsequent articles in *New Left Review*, in the tradition of the World Systems School founded by Immanuel Wallerstein, a new path-breaking book on China's emergence as the challenger to United States' world hegemony. Despite the book's title, Adam Smith does not really get to Beijing until page 267 of the 389 pages of text. The great bulk of the book brings up to date (2007) Arrighi's thesis of the succession of world capitalist systems of Venice, Genoa, Holland, Britain, ending with the United States, each having a productive beginning leading to financial domination. In this thesis Arrighi emphasises the importance of the military power which wealth bestowed, and was the basis of imperial expansion. While Marx and Engels wrote of cheap commodities as the 'heavy artillery' with which the European bourgeoisie 'batter down all Chinese walls', Arrighi emphasises that 'British cotton cloth could never compete in Chinese rural markets with stronger Chinese cloth'. It was British gunboats and opium that conquered China.

In Arrighi's world systems, Britain's industrial revolution and the emergence of industrial capitalism, based on the power of capital and the exploitation of wage labour, are seen as secondary to Britain's displacement of 'Amsterdam as the financial centre of the globalising European system of states'. This is how Arrighi writes of the 1780s, the very years of Britain's industrialisation. Britain thus became, in Arrighi's view, 'the heir of the imperialist tradition initiated by the Iberian partners of the Genoese'. British industry's scouring of the world for raw materials and for markets for its manufactures is thus seen as the product rather than the source of its financial power. This all seems to sit rather awkwardly with the central argument over the causes of boom and slump in the 1920s-30s, and again in the 1950s-70s, which Arrighi conducts with Robert Brenner throughout the book. Brenner is accused of over-emphasising the competition between rival industrial powers, and under-emphasising the conflicts between capital and labour. I would agree, but on a 'World Systems' view the rise of the United States to world hegemony, or at least to domination over the European powers, would seem to be more significant.

The core chapters of Arrighi's new book concern the inability of the

United States to move from military domination to hegemony. Arrighi sees this not only as the result of the military failure in Iraq, but of mistaken policies of raw militaristic imperialism offered by the 'Neo-Cons' that led to the Iraq invasion. He titles the core chapter 11 'The World State that Never Was', and spells out the alternative that could have made the United States into a world state. This he takes from David Harvey's *The New Imperialism* as a sort of New Deal led by the United States and Europe:

> 'This means liberating the logic of capital ... from its neo-liberal chains, reformulating state powers along much more interventionist and redistributive lines, curbing the speculative powers of finance capital, and decentralising or democratically controlling the overwhelming power of oligopolies and monopolies (in particular ... of the military-industrial complex).'

This alternative project, Arrighi comments, resembles the 'ultra-imperialism' of co-operating European powers envisaged long ago by Karl Kautsky, but he insists that it also corresponds to Adam Smith's picture of an ultimate reconciliation of his 'natural' and 'un-natural' forms of development, through the demise in hopeless contradictions of the latter. And this eventuality is obviously what inspires Arrighi in considering the outcome of the Chinese challenge to the United States.

Arrighi's introduction of Adam Smith's thought about 'natural' and 'un-natural' development enables him to build on the self-destructive essence of industrial capitalism to reveal a possible outcome in China for 'industrious' capitalism, that is one that is based on human labour at its centre and not on labour saving and exploitation, together with capital-rich machinery. But, first, he is anxious to reveal the real threat to US claims to world hegemony – and this was written before the financial collapse of 2008-9. Arrighi, rightly in my view, puts his finger not only on the enormous military cost to the United States and utter failure of the Iraq invasion, but also on the relative decline of US manufacturing industry. The United States was unable to pay its bills, and became totally dependent on Chinese and East Asian finance. This was the moment when the United States' claim to world hegemony collapsed, and the so-called 'peaceful ascent' of China became a real threat to the US.

How the US might respond to this challenge becomes the subject of Arrighi's last chapters, but first he explores the reality of China's market based 'industrious' capitalism. More than I have read anywhere else, Arrighi emphasises the labour intensive nature of Chinese industry, the absence of capital-intensive robots in Chinese manufacturing, and the huge importance of non-agricultural production in rural China. A major difference from European economic development through the dispossession of the peasantry was the destruction in China of the power of the landlord class and the redistributive land reforms. This had begun under Mao in the 1940s, and Arrighi reminds us how important for China's subsequent economic development was the foundation created by the communes and decentralisation of the Mao years. Even the mad Cultural Revolution to some extent undermined the bureaucracy of the Communist Party, and brought the urban middle classes to recognise the capacities of the rural population. China's rapid economic development under Deng was based essentially on the domestic economy and local control of agricultural surpluses. In fact, the success of the Township and Village Enterprises (TVEs) in the 1990s was so great that even Deng himself declared them to be 'totally out of our expectations'. They have not ended the vast gap in incomes and wealth between urban and rural societies.

This is where Arrighi sees Adam Smith in Beijing. Smith would have encouraged the 'natural' path of development through agricultural improvement and domestic trade. Far from leaving trade and industry to the free working of market forces, as many modern free marketeers would now cite Smith as their authority, Smith himself believed profoundly in the need of the legislator to regulate the market in the general interest. This is quite evidently, according to Arrighi, what the Chinese Communist Party has been doing. As Arrighi explains Chinese official development policy:

> 'They make capitalists, rather than workers, compete with one another, so that profits are driven down to a minimum tolerable level. They encourage division of labour among, rather than within, production units and communities, and invest in education to counter the negative effects of the division of labour on the intellectual qualities of the population.'

To take one example, the establishment of huge Export Processing Zones (EPZs), far from simply adopting and adapting foreign giant company investment, has been combined, as Arrighi writes, 'with the transformation of several Chinese cities into hotbeds of technical research' and 'an expansion of the educational system at a pace and on a scale without precedent even in East Asia'.

When Arrighi comes to consider how the United States might respond to the Chinese challenge, he examines three alternatives. The first is a direct confrontation, perhaps starting with Taiwan, leading almost inevitably to a war which neither humanity nor the planet can afford. The second is a delaying game of playing off China and her potential allies – Russia, India, Japan and the rest of West Asia – against each other and remaining aloof until the last minute, as the US did in the two World Wars. The third, which Arrighi evidently hopes for, is that of a new 'Bandung' reproducing the treaty of non-alignment of the 1950s. This could only follow from a further strengthening of Chinese industrious development, and weakening of industrial development elsewhere. Arrighi fears, however, that the Chinese élite might still become a new bourgeoisie, and turn towards Smith's 'unnatural' development with all the disastrous results in growing inequality and ecological breakdown that this would entail. The role of Europe and of a new US President would be crucial in this conjuncture, but despite an unprecedented world financial crisis, it seems that from these quarters we can only expect more of the same which produced the crisis. Can the Chinese rescue us, not just financially, but by their socialism?

Michael Barratt Brown

The Biggest Organ

Ffion Hague, *The Pain and the Pleasure: The Women in Lloyd George's Life*, Harper Press, hardback ISBN 9780007219400, £25

When I was invited to review Ffion Hague's text, I hesitated. I had not heard of her as an historian but as William Hague's partner. I expected a pot-boiler written with a right-wing slant. I procrastinated but agreed to receive a copy of the publisher's blurb, which lead me to agree. I was glad I did.

Despite committing myself to read 590 plus pages, which ate into time I should have been giving to other commitments, I have no regrets. One should never rely on one's prejudices. I was mistaken on a number of counts. The values implicit in her treatment of L.G. and the period are the ones I am inclined to share.

Ffion Hague explores and empathises with the lives of the numerous women who loved Lloyd George. She has written a revealing and fascinating text enriched by her own judicious comments and exploration of her subject's motives. L.G. was a serial womaniser with, it appears, an excess of libido. His Principal Private Secretary, A. J. Sylvester, who knew L.G. and his family over a number of years, describes L.G. getting out of his bath in 1931 – he was then 65 years of age. He wrote admiringly in his diary: 'There he stood ... with the biggest organ I have ever seen. It resembles a donkey's ... It must be a sight for the Gods – or the women – in erection! No wonder they are always after him and he after them!' Elsewhere he records the comment: 'If L.G. gave his mind to thinking how he could best help the country, instead of thinking cunt and women, he would be a better man.' The author's meticulous research of contemporary documents demonstrates that Sylvester was correct about L.G.'s sexual proclivity. He had two wives and innumerable sexual partners ...

Contemporary observers claim he had an hypnotic effect on women.

He married his first wife, Maggie, in 1888; 25 years later, in 1913, he 'married' his second wife, Frances Stevenson. He was then 50. Much of the text records in intimate and revealing detail the manner in which L.G. succeeded in managing to keep his affair with Frances Stevenson from public scrutiny in what we would now regard as a censorious age. The author has the good fortune of being able to access voluminous archival material, which enables her to describe in detail the manner in which he was able to conceal his relationships from his wife and family. Matters were facilitated by Frances acting as one of his Private Secretaries.

I strongly recommend Ffion Hague's text for readers wishing to enlighten themselves as to the value system of their Welsh forebears. Readers will be aware of the changes in public attitudes in respect of sexual and relationship norms during the nineteenth century, and be surprised to read that L.G. was able to survive the damaging gossip and reports of his philandering. He was able to do so, relying on his wife's public testimony. What will come as a surprise is Ffion Hague's recording of the intensity of religious belief, and the schism among members of the non-conformist community. We learn that when L.G. was married, his father-in-law would not hear of his daughter being married in a Baptist chapel, whereas his uncle, to whom he was devoted, would not countenance a Methodist wedding. After much discussion, a compromise was eventually agreed.

I was also struck by an account she gives of the ethnic divide in North Wales and the attempts to abnegate the Welsh language. She records the level of retribution inflicted on a member of L.G.'s family who, when at school, spoke to a schoolmate in Welsh. She records that his teacher struck him on the side of his head with such force that he permanently lost his hearing in one ear.

Hague reminds her readers of L.G.'s radical past, and gives details of his famous 1909-1910 'People's Budget'. He proposed raising thirteen million pounds more in taxes – a massive sum by today's standards. The rich would pay more income tax, inheritance tax would be increased, and drinkers and smokers would pay more for their supposed pleasures. His most radical proposal was a system of land taxes.

The author reminds her readers that L.G. opposed the Anglo-Boer War. He was acutely conscious of the fact that the war was costing enormous sums, which would have paid for measures to tackle poverty at home. In one of his speeches L.G. noted that there was not a shell which burst on an African hill that did not carry away an old age pension. Challenging his audience, he asked: 'What is the satisfaction? Oh, it killed two hundred Boers – fathers of families, sons of mothers, who wept for them. Are you satisfied to give your old age pension for that?'

L.G.'s reputation, which he gained as a radical Chancellor of the Exchequer and war-time Premier, was compromised by his alleged abuse of the honours system. From Hague's account, it appears that both the Liberal and Conservative Parties benefited from the sale of honours.

Under Asquith's leadership, the Liberal Party amassed a sum of £1.5 million – £59 million in today's value. The going rate for a knighthood was £12,000 (which could be paid in instalments) and £35,000 for a baronetcy. L.G. did not deny the practice. He claimed it was preferable to the American system, when the steel trusts supported one party and cotton interests another. He argued that giving money to a political party should not rule out someone from receiving an honour.

I have just one niggle: commenting on changes in Britain's social structure in the Edwardian period. Ffion Hague writes of contraception being 'readily available'. I question, as will others, this proposition. One final comment: the author has produced a text of considerable merit. Moreover, the value of the book is greatly enhanced by the inclusion of a Victorian style index, which will be of inestimable assistance to scholars working on the period in question. It is worth anyone's twenty-five pounds. I hope it appears in paperback.

Peter M. Jackson

Financial Hegemon?

Martin Wolf, *Fixing Global Finance: How to Curb Financial Crises in the 21st Century,* Yale University Press, New Haven and London, 230 pages, ISBN 9780300142778, £18.99

This is certainly not a political economy analysis of financial crises, or even a structured critique of the role of finance in economies. The author is a subscriber to the 'globalisation does us good' school. Chapter 1 kicks off with 'Finance is the brain of the market economy' (p.1). There is no reference to corruption, ENRON, pension mis-selling, the dissembling presentations of banks, Savings and Loans companies, insurance and mortgage companies, stock markets, and the failed theory of private pensions leading to economic growth and greater individual security (variously, Ghilarducci, and Kay and Sinha in references below). The book fizzles out at the end with no real policy changes.

But once we understand where the author is coming from, some fascinating questions emerge. Pursuing the biological or anatomical analogies of much recent economics, he comments that 'The brain is susceptible to a variety of infirmities' (also page 1). Then he refers to Charles Kindleberger and Andrew Glyn (references below), both radical commentators with invaluable contributions to the story of finance. The author is well read and the bibliography alone is worth the read.

The main argument is this; how has the United States become the 'spender and borrower of last resort', piling up massive foreign debt, much of it supplied by so-called developing countries who could get a better rate of return domestically? It is not just about US financial supremacy, but also about international politics based on the dollar as the measure of value. The conventional economic development theory is that the flow of funds should be the other way around, developed to developing countries. But developing countries (China and India in particular) are funding the profligacy of the super-power.

Wolf has an excellent section on the 'pyramids of promises' (p. 11ff). 'Sophisticated and dynamic modern economies depend on pyramids of promises' (p.12). But it all depends on that elusive concept (my words) called 'trust'. The author notes that the degree of trust necessary to sustain the system has been rare. 'That is at least part of the reason why financial crises have been so frequent and so dangerous' (p. 13).

According to Wolf, it is about the denomination of the debt. The old adage, 'if you owe the bank 10 quid, you're in trouble, but if you owe a million, they are', is overtaken by 'it depends what currency you are dealing in'. So the underlying thesis of the book (my words again) is about the fickle role of the all-important dollar following the expense of the Vietnam war, its devaluation and the incompetence of the corrupt Nixon administration. This is all very well, however. It is hard to understand why such a monetary unit is still so dominant, and why developing, including Muslim countries, want it, especially when it probably contributes to US subsidies and guarantees of Israeli debt and weapons purchases from the US to occupy Palestine, kill Muslim men, women and children, maintain nuclear weapons, and export arms to questionable regimes. We, or they, fail to make these connections. Money and its supposed neutrality – solely a means of exchange – take on other, political implications.

The role of the United States, and its personification in a currency, is the theme of the book, and a perceptive one. My main complaint is that one has to plough through page after page of figures, tables, charts, descriptions about current/capital account surpluses/deficits, currency liabilities, exchange rates and much else besides, all of which are necessary, but spoil the plot. Much of these could be put in appendices.

Now to the final conclusions and questions. 'The performance of the financial system has been the Achilles heel of the era of globalisation' (p. 195). 'How plausible are these arguments for the sustainability of the pattern of capital flows from the world at large to the world's richest country?' (p. 136). 'The answer is a global one: a large number of countries have been unable to absorb their savings at home, even at low real rates of interest' (p.63). And that is the nub of the issue. The question remains, why not? And that is political, not economic.

The book ends with a considered critique of the International Monetary Fund, and a passing of responsibility back to individual countries themselves. But surely there is much more to be said about the role of finance, and the US – the financial hegemon – in international development. The author has made a good shot at it, but the attempt is rather apolitical, albeit interesting in its own terms. I do not think he convinces us about 'fixing global finance' or 'curbing financial crises'. My own conclusion is that until finance is defined as a public utility, with national and international organisations to treat it as such, the sorry saga will continue.

Richard Minns

References
Ghilarducci, Teresa, *When I'm Sixty-Four; The Plot Against Pensions and the Plan to Save Them,* Princeton, 2008
Glyn, Andrew, *Capitalism Unleashed; Finance, Globalisation and Welfare,* OUP, 2006
Kay, Stephen, and Tapen Shina, *Lessons from Pension Reform in the Americas,* Oxford, 2008
Kindleburger, Charles, and Robert Aliber, *Manias, Panics and Crashes; A History of Financial Crises,* Palgrave, 2005

America's End

Gabriel Kolko, *World in Crisis: The End of the American Century*, Pluto Press, 190 pages, paperback ISBN 9780745328652, £12.99

Gabriel Kolko was writing about the global financial crisis long before it hit. In 2006, he wrote in this journal 'There has been a profound and fundamental change in the world economy over the past decade. The very triumph of liberalization and deregulation ... has also produced a deepening crisis that its advocates scarcely expected' ('Crisis of Greed' *Spokesman 92*). Now the world is mired in slump, and all around there are claims that no one saw it coming. Kolko has reason to differ.

His new book is about the end of the American century. This is a telling counterblast to the neoconservative claims to a New American Century, which have proved so hollow. Kolko gives chapter and verse on those failures. He writes:

> 'All of Bush's major policies, especially his wars in Afghanistan and Iraq and the grandiose neoconservative agenda to make the US the dominant world power, have failed, leaving a legacy of fear and hatred in the Middle East and much of the rest of the world, while making an enemy of Russia and weakening America's traditional alliances.'

The folly of America's overseas misadventures compounds its acute economic decline. Wars in Afghanistan and Iraq have been 'costly beyond imagination, will endure long after those who begun them leave Washington, and yet will end in failure.'

According to Kolko, 'US foreign policy has always suffered from a disjunction between policy and reality ... the way it treats fictions as facts – and why – has been crucial in shaping the demise of its immense power.' This brings to mind the extraordinary deceits shared by Bush and Blair in bringing 'shock and awe' to the people of Iraq. A bigger pair of liars would be hard to find.

Kolko is the historian for everyman. He ranges across America's lamentable record on the world stage during the Twentieth Century. In plain words, he spells out the pressing limits on those who gave us the horrors of 'full spectrum dominance', while eschewing such brutal jargon himself. He sums up the United States' demise thus:

> 'Nothing quite illustrates the end of American power so well as its strategy in the Middle East – where it has sustained Israel, made war in Iraq, and tried several times since 1954 (successfully in that case) to overthrow Teheran governments.'

This little book should be on everyone's wish list.

Anthony Lane

Afan Valley

Tina Carr and Annemarie Schöne, *Coalfaces – Life After Coal in the Afan Valley*, Parthian Books Cardigan, 82 pages including 51 full page colour prints, hardback ISBN 9781905762545, £19-99 with DVD

The landscapes and architecture shown in these colour prints make it clear that life in a remote Welsh valley was not easy even before the pit closures. If you like pictures with your politics you may appreciate this sociological visual inquiry into the lives of the inhabitants of the upper Afan valley, some 15 miles inland from Port Talbot on the coast of South Wales. This valley, carved by the river into the post-glacial peneplane from a height of almost 2,000 feet, surprisingly is not a blind one. Its road with several hairpin bends connects with the Rhondda valley to the east.

The book, like all the photographs, is landscape in format, and there is narrative including a postscript by the authors in which they explain their interests in the social and ecological effects of industry and big business, and their preference for the philosophy of E F Schumacher. The two author-artist-photographers are introduced by Amanda Hopkinson, a journalist and academic with Welsh connections, and by Osi Rhys Osmond, an artist, writer, teacher and broadcaster born of a mining family in the Sirhowy valley. Both rightly applaud the commitment, concern and sensitivity of the authors. Osmond's comment on the effects of 20 years of pit closures is quoted below. The effects include 65% male unemployment in some areas.

'They have become a people stranded by history as the great wealth of the coalfield bypassed the communities that produced it leaving them with deep social and physical scars, powerful collective memories and an extraordinary and very necessary social resilience in the face of the constructive indifference of the political élites.'

The greater indifference was that of the Thatcher government, which irrationally sacrificed the industry to achieve the greater objective of disabling a powerful trade union as an object lesson to all others. Mrs Thatcher cared little for the fact that no democracy is safe without democratic trade unions, and she was later a defender of General Augusto Pinochet. She probably knew nothing of the grandparents of people such as those photographed in this book, some of who saw fascism taking root in Europe before her party did, and who went to Spain to try to halt it.

Christopher Gifford

Fabricator

Bob Drogin, *Curveball: Spies, lies, and the man behind them – The real reason America went to war in Iraq*, Ebury Press, 444 pages, paperback ISBN 9780091923044, £6.99

'The intelligence and facts were being fixed around the policy.' That was the chilling message Sir Richard Dearlove, then head of the British intelligence organisation MI6, brought back from Washington in July 2002, eight months before the land invasion of Iraq.

The leaked minute, which became widely known as the 'Downing Street Memo', records Sir Richard ('C') telling his fellow spooks, sundry assistants to Tony Blair, as well as Jack Straw (Foreign Secretary) and Geoff Hoon (Defence Secretary) that it's countdown to war. It reads:

> 'C reported on his recent talks in Washington. There was a perceptible shift in attitude. Military action was now seen as inevitable. Bush wanted to remove Saddam, through military action, justified by the conjunction of terrorism and WMD. *But the intelligence and facts were being fixed around the policy [emphasis added]*. The National Security Council had no patience with the UN route, and no enthusiasm for publishing material on the Iraqi regime's record. There was little discussion in Washington of the aftermath after military action.'

Surprisingly, neither the Downing Street Memo, nor the excellent website it gave rise to in the United States (downingstreetmemo.com), are mentioned in Mr Drogin's book. Tony Blair rates one mention, as does David Kelly, the British expert on chemical and biological weapons who was found dead on the day Mr Blair was originally to have received his Presidential Medal of Freedom in Washington. (It was finally hung round Blair's neck on 13 January 2009, at the bitter end of Bush's second term).

For *Curveball* claims to reveal 'the real reason America went to war in Iraq'. But it does nothing of the kind. The British spook, Dearlove, does a better job in the quotation above. What the real imperatives were that drove the decision to invade and occupy Iraq is a far more complex question which still awaits a proper answer. But the thesis here seems to be that a lone Iraqi chancer who claimed asylum in Germany, and was codenamed 'Curveball' by the Germans intelligence service who guarded him jealously, somehow duped the US intelligence, military and political brass by claiming active involvement in the construction of mobile laboratories to produce biological and chemical weapons. His claims were the basis of Bush's reference to Iraqi mobile labs in his 2003 State of the Union speech. Curveball's drawings prefigured the diagrams Colin Powell flashed up in the UN Security Council chamber as he argued for shock and awe in Iraq. (See *Spokesman 86*.)

These claims were complete bunkum. They were totally bogus, as David Kelly confirmed in the months before his untimely death. Indeed, they were as baseless as Blair's claims about Iraq's ability to launch nuclear, chemical and biological weapons within 45 minutes of an order to do so. David Kelly also tried to expose those lies.

Curveball, an Iraqi taxi driver, was finally interviewed by United States officials in March 2004, when the analyst was able to confirm that he was, indeed, a 'fabricator'. He wasn't the only one.

Tony Simpson

Fly on the Wall

Joachim C. Fest, *Albert Speer: Conversations with Hitler's Architect***, Polity Press, 180 pages, hardback ISBN 9780745639185, £19.99**

Of all the biographer's and writers on the Third Reich, Joachim Fest was not only good at his craft, but also had the good fortune to be invited to act, as he describes it, as 'interrogating editor' for the best selling autobiography of Albert Speer, the highest ranking Nazi to escape a death sentence at the Nuremburg Trials. This book is no heavy biography, which Fest completed earlier. No, what he has done is to create the literary equivalent of a fly-on-the-wall documentary.

In this book Fest records, at his own personal level, the numerous significant encounters he had with Speer, frequently accompanied by Wolf Jobst Siedler, the editor of the publishing house who won the contract for Speer's memoirs. The effect of this style is to make readers feel that they are on the inside track, almost to the point of wishing to ask their own questions at times.

The search for a single cause of the madness that was the Third Reich is, of course, as elusive as ever, what with the vanities, lust for power, and the threat of the firing squad hanging over anyone who stepped over a none-too-well defined line. That line would ultimately be defined by Hitler himself, should defining be required, even post hoc. Add to this the internal struggles, and Hitler's inner circle could be likened to ferrets in a sack. Within this was Albert Speer, Hitler's architect, who rose to be his munitions minister in 1942.

Speer's trial and his approach to his pleas of mitigation describe the incredible turmoil that must have been within Speer's head. He was convinced that the death sentence was to be his fate after the court had been shown the American news film of the concentration camps. At some point he decided to fight, and it is suggested that the shock of finding himself in the dock with such mass murderers as Kaltenbrunner or Frank, and characters like Streicher, made him realise that, for his own spiritual survival, he had to distance himself from them. For his trouble he escaped death, but earned scorn from others, particularly those detained in Spandau.

Fest himself was always troubled by Hitler's final denouement in his Berlin bunker. It was difficult for him to reconcile Speer with his decision to make a last visit to Hitler. Yet, at a meeting between the Fest and Speer in September 1974, Speer finally opened up on this crucial visit. What is revealed is a scene of mayhem where even the plumbing stopped functioning. It also reveals how the power of the Führer had faded in that, although he was confronted by insubordination on the part of Speer, he allowed it to pass.

Almost as an aside, Fest drops into his account an indication of the vanity and sense of possession that can exist between biographers and their subjects. Frau Gitta Sereny, who was also interested in the Speers, had arranged a meeting with Speer's son, who is also called Albert. On discovering that Fest was accompanying Albert Junior, Sereny threw a small fit and refused to attend the meeting as she wanted it to be one to one. As it happened, Fest had taken the trouble to bring with him the notes which formed the basis of this book, fully intending to give them to Sereny to aid her work. I wonder if she has ever realised the service she did to the recorded history of these times by ensuring Fest himself wrote up the notes.

Henry McCubbin

Thriller

Carl Tighe, *Druids Hill*, Five Leaves Publications, 168 pages, paperback ISBN 9781905512553, £7.99

In September 1973, the recently appointed Commander-in-Chief of the Chilean Army, General Augusto Pinochet, led a *coup d'état* against President Salvador Allende. The coup was successful, and Pinochet remained in office until 1990. Almost immediately after securing power, Pinochet banned all leftist parties that had been associated with Allende's government. The dictator's violence was not just aimed at political parties alone, but towards any dissident, their family and other civilians too. In all it is believed that nearly 3,000 people disappeared, 30,000 were tortured, and several thousands were exiled whilst Pinochet was President of Chile.

On a cold wintry day in 1975, a young boy is delivering newspapers to an old mansion when he notices something unusual and enters the house. Upon discovering the house's contents, he is blasted with a shotgun and dies immediately. Then, 25 years later, in 2000, a man dies at a demonstration in Manchester against General Pinochet. Could the murdered teenager, the death at the demonstration, and the *coup d'état* in Chile be linked somehow?

Druids Hill is a crime thriller set in Manchester. It follows Emma Tulip, a journalist, as she investigates the contents of the mansion on Druids Hill, which led to the death of the fourteen-year-old boy. She discovers two mysterious characters, Miller and Agard, who, before their deaths, hid information proving that the CIA was closely involved with Pinochet's coup. Several sinister characters would like to get hold of this information, but Emma beats them to it. Can she escape the same fate as the paperboy, Miller and Agard, and the hapless man at the demonstration?

Carl Tighe's novel is a fast-paced political thriller that entwines fact with fiction. Throughout, the main narrative is interspersed with the chronology of General Pinochet's rise to power. It is a fascinating read, which delves into corruption, restricted information and murder, within the world of the novel as well as the real world itself.

Abi Rhodes

A Communication from Florida

'My copy of *The Island That Dared* [reviewed in *Spokesman 102*] has not been sitting idle for a minute. It is a very hot number, being passed around as fast as anyone can finish it, with a waiting list of people eager to read it. If you folks are in touch with Dervla Murphy, please tell her how much her new book is appreciated here in Central Florida where a number of our peace and justice folks went to Cuba (at considerable risk) in the mid to late 1990s on friendship tours and others of us sent clothes, medical supplies, and other stuff through Pastors for Peace. Thanks again for your review, which alerted me to the book.'

Joyce Chumbley

Bakers, Food & Allied Workers Union

Supporting workers in struggle Wherever they may be.

Joe Marino   General Secretary
Ronnie Draper   President
Jackie Barnwell Vice President

Stanborough House,
Great North Road,
Stanborough,
Welwyn Garden City,
Hertfordshire. AL8 7TA

Phone 01707 260150 & 01707 259450
www.bfawu.org

Fighting for Trade Union freedom

Build peace not bombs

Bob Crow
General Secretary

John Leach
President

scottish left review

Since 2000 the Scottish Left Review has been Scotland's leading journal of radical politics. It is non-party but aims to provide a space for ideas and debate for those on the Left of all parties and none.

Read current issues and subscribe at

www.scottishleftreview.org

THE BERTRAND RUSSELL PEACE FOUNDATION
DOSSIER

US 'ASSASSINATION RING' – SEYMOUR HERSH

On 10 March 2009 at the University of Minnesota, the investigative reporter Seymour Hersh and former US Vice President Walter Mondale addressed a public meeting on 'America's Constitutional Crisis'. They discussed how presidents are drawn into covert actions that exceed their constitutional powers, apparently believing that they can get results and will never be found out. At the end of one answer by Hersh about how these things happen, the Chairman asked: 'And do they continue to happen to this day?' Hersh replied:

'Yes. After 9/11, I haven't written about this yet, but the Central Intelligence Agency was very deeply involved in domestic activities against people they thought to be enemies of the state. Without any legal authority for it. They haven't been called on it yet. That does happen.

Right now, today, there was a story in the *New York Times* that, if you read it carefully, mentioned something known as the Joint Special Operations Command – JSOC it's called. It is a special wing of our special operations community that is set up independently. They do not report to anybody, except in the Bush-Cheney days, they reported directly to the Cheney office. They did not report to the chairman of the joint chiefs of staff or to Mr. [Robert] Gates, the secretary of defense. They reported directly to him ... Congress has no oversight of it. It's an executive assassination ring essentially, and it's been going on and on and on. Just today, in the *Times* there was a story that its leader, a three star admiral named [William H.] McRaven, ordered a stop to it because there were so many collateral deaths. Under President Bush's authority, they've been going into countries, not talking to the ambassador or the CIA station chief, and finding people on a list and executing them and leaving. That's been going on, in the name of all of us.

It's complicated because the guys doing it are not murderers, and yet they are committing what we would normally call murder. It's a very complicated issue. Because they are young men that went into the Special Forces. The Delta Forces you've heard about. Navy Seal teams. Highly specialized. In many cases, they were the best and the brightest. Really, no exaggerations. Really fine guys that went in to do the kind of necessary jobs that they think you need to do to protect America. And then they find themselves torturing people.

I've had people say to me – five years ago, I had one say: "What do you call it when you interrogate somebody and you leave them bleeding and they don't get any medical committee and two days later he dies. Is that murder? What happens if I get before a committee?"

But they're not going to get before a committee.'

In July 2008 in *The New Yorker*, Seymour Hersh wrote about the Joint Special Operations Command. He said:

'Under the Bush Administration's interpretation of the law, clandestine military activities, unlike covert CIA operations, do not need to be depicted in a Finding*, because the President has a constitutional right to command combat forces in the field without congressional interference.'

Other matters raised during the meeting included:
- The My Lai massacre, which Hersh first revealed publicly.
- The Pentagon Papers case, which Mondale described as the best example of the 'government's potential for vast public deception'.
- Henry Kissinger's secret dealings, mostly relating to the Vietnam War.
- The Church Committee investigation of CIA and FBI abuses, in which Mondale played a major role.
- The Iran Contra scandal. (Hersh said the Reagan administration came to office with a clear goal of finding a way to finance covert actions, such as the funding of the Nicaraguan Contras, without appropriations so that Congress wouldn't know about them. Mondale noted that Reagan had signed a law barring further aid to the Contras, then participated in a scheme to keep the aid flowing. Hersh said that two key veterans of Iran-Contra, Dick Cheney and national security official Elliot Abrams, were reunited in the George W. Bush White House and decided that the key lesson from Iran-Contra was that too many people in the administration knew about it.)
- And the Bush-Cheney years. (Hersh said: 'The contempt for Congress in the Bush-Cheney White House was extaordinary.' Mondale said of his successor, Cheney, and his inner circle: 'they ran a government within the government'. Hersh added: 'Eight or nine neoconservatives took over our country'. Mondale said that the precedents of abuse of vice presidential power by Cheney would remain 'like a loaded pistol that you leave on the dining room table'.)

*'Finding' refers to a special document that a president must issue, although not make public, to authorise covert CIA actions.

The 'beautiful thing about our system' is that eventually we get new leaders, Hersh said. 'The evil twosome, Cheney and Bush, left.' But he also said 'it's really amazing to me that we manage to get such bad leadership, so consistently'. And he added that both the press and the public let down their guard in the aftermath of 9/11. 'The major newspapers joined the [Bush] team,' Hersh said. Top editors passed the message to investigative reporters not to 'pick holes' in what Bush was doing. Violations of the Bill of Rights happened in the plain sight of the public. It it was not only tolerated, but Bush was re-elected.

With grateful acknowledgements to Eric Black and the Minnesota Post.

Independent Thinking from Polity

MAX WEBER
A BIOGRAPHY

Joachim Radkau, *Bielefeld University*

'Joachim Radkau is the first biographer to bring the great social thinker Max Weber to life. He reveals what others tried to conceal: the emotional turmoil suffered by the champion of rationality.' Lord Dahrendorf

Radkau brings out, in a way that no one has ever done before, the intimate interrelations between Weber's thought and his life experience. He presents detailed revelations about the great enigmas of Weber's life: his suffering and erotic experiences, his fears and his desires, his creative power and his methods of work as well as his religious experience and his relation to nature and to death. By understanding the great drama of his life, we discover a new Max Weber, until now unknown in many respects, and, at the same time, we gain a new appreciation of his work.

700 pages | January 2009
ISBN: 978-0-7456-4147-8
hb £25.00

To order, phone John Wiley & Sons Ltd free on 0800 243407
www.politybooks.com

WORLD PREMIERE
A New World by Trevor Griffiths
29 August – 9 October 2009
at **Shakespeare's Globe, London**

A play about Thomas Paine, revolutionary and author of *The Rights of Man*, on his bicentenary

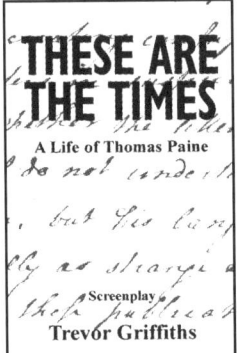

These Are The Times:
A Life of Thomas Paine
Screenplay by Trevor Griffiths

'reads like the greatest of novels and is the most thrilling read I have had in years. It is a gorgeous pagent of American idealism.' **Kurt Vonnegut**

'politically searching, dramatically compelling and superbly entertaining ... does more to retrieve one of England's most magnificent radicals than anything that has ever been done before.' **Terry Eagleton**

Price £15.00 - ISBN: 978 0 85124 6956

Theatre Plays Vols. One and Two
By Trevor Griffiths

The collected edition of all Trevor Griffiths' work for the theatre.

"Trevor Griffiths is the godfather of British political theatre ... our foremost socialist dramatist.'
Michael Billington,
The Guardian

The Wages of Thin | Sam, Sam
Occupations | Apricots | Thermidor
The Party | Comedians
The Cherry Orchard

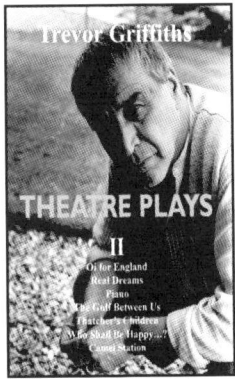

Oi for England | Real Dreams
Piano | The Gulf between Us
Thatcher's Children | Who shall be
Happy ... ? | Camel Station

Price £15.00 each - 1 - 978 085124 7205 | 2 - 978 085124 7212 | pb

---

Spokesman Books, Russell House, Nottingham, NG6 0BT, England
Tel: 0115 9708318 - Fax: 0115 9420433 - elfeuro@compuserve.com
Order online at www.spokesmanbooks.com